COGNITIVE THERAPY

COGNITIVE THERAPY

Transforming the Image

Frank Wills
and
Diana Sanders

SAGE Publications
London • Thousand Oaks • New Delhi

First published 1997
Reprinted 2000, 2002, 2003

 SAGE Publications Ltd
6 Bonhill Street
London EC2A 4PU

SAGE Publications Inc
2455 Teller Road
Thousand Oaks, California 91320

SAGE Publications India Pvt Ltd
32, M-Block Market
Greater Kailash – I
New Delhi 110 048

British Library Cataloguing in Publication data

A catalogue record for this book is available from
the British Library

ISBN 0 7619 5082 6
ISBN 0 7619 5083 4 (pbk)

Library of Congress catalog card number 97–068916

Typeset by Photoprint, Torquay, Devon
Printed in Great Britain by Biddles Ltd, www.Biddles.co.uk

Contents

Preface

The cognitive approach to counselling has a long-standing tendency to be the poor relation of the counselling world. Many counsellors still hold an image of cognitive therapy that is coldly rational and unimaginatively mechanistic in its methods and have felt a degree of resistance to the cognitive model. This may be partly due to the fact that cognitive therapy is such a recent arrival on the counselling scene and, as yet, only a relatively small cohort of skilled trainers has emerged. Often trainees on a counselling course will be taught cognitive concepts by tutors with little enthusiasm for, or real knowledge of, the model. Cognitive therapy has, in recent years, undergone massive changes which transcend many of the previously held criticisms. *Cognitive Therapy: Transforming the Image* aims, as the title suggests, to transform the negative image of the cognitive model by describing not only cognitive therapy's original methods, but also the wave of therapeutic creativity which is sweeping through it. The book aims to give counsellors greater interest in entering the treasure house of methods and concepts which have been shown to be so effective in many therapeutic areas. The overall cognitive framework within which this variety of methods can be used is represented in the concept of the 'cognitive case conceptualisation'. Within this framework, traditional cognitive techniques such as behavioural experiments and challenging dysfunctional thinking can take place. Case conceptualisation also gives an overall cognitive rationale to some of the newer interests of cognitive therapists: working with emotions; giving a high profile to the therapeutic relationship; working with images and other non-verbal aspects; and working with deeper core beliefs relating back to early and other formative experiences. We describe this widening horizon of theory and practice and the ever-widening scope of the client issues to which the cognitive approach can be applied. The aim is not to give a prescriptive manual but rather to give a flavour of cognitive therapy and how it may be used by counsellors.

The Introduction to the book aims to persuade the reader to give cognitively based counselling a chance. It begins by anticipating the reader's reservations and explaining how many of the objections to cognitive therapy have already been met by recent developments in the field. After the Introduction, each of the chapters of Part I explains the original cognitive model, and updates it with current developments. Cognitive case conceptualisation and newer approaches to the therapeutic relationship in cognitive therapy are then described in detail. The second part of the book aims to show how the theoretical principles described in Part I are operationalised into the working methods of cognitive therapy. Different stages of the process are described using examples from our casebooks to illustrate the process in action. Part II describes how to commence cognitive therapy, including issues of engaging the client and assessment. A chapter follows on the nuts and bolts of cognitive therapy and how to integrate the technical aspects of therapy into the conceptualisation. The next chapter describes schema-focused cognitive therapy, which aims to work with client's deeply held beliefs, using a greater emphasis on the therapeutic relationship and a variety of methods which are in many ways likely to be familiar to many counsellors. Part II concludes with common difficulties with cognitive therapy. What happens when the therapy does not fit the client or his or her problems? Or if the client goes through the motions of therapy but does not feel better? These and other issues are addressed. The third and final part of the book addresses integration of cognitive therapy into the counselling world. Some readers who have enjoyed this book may still be wondering how they might begin to use some or all of the techniques and concepts described herein within their present working style. We end with a special consideration of the use of cognitive theory and practice specifically in *counselling*, highlighting three ways of using cognitive therapy in practice. The first strategy would be to use some of the cognitive concepts and skills in a highly eclectic way – having, for example, the use of a thought record as one of a series of highly diverse tools in a therapy toolbag. The second strategy is to seek a fuller training in cognitive therapy and to attempt to implement a largely cognitive approach under supervision. The final strategy is to look more seriously at how the cognitive model and its methods could be fitted into the counsellor's existing work, in line with the integrative approaches to psychotherapy.

Notes on case studies and language: The case vignettes are based on our clients, but all identifying details have been changed. We have used the male and female pronouns at random throughout the book, unless referring to specific clients. We use the term 'cognitive therapy' to refer to the tradition that has developed from the work of Aaron T. Beck. This is not intended to ignore the important contributions of other authors within the cognitive-behavioural field such as those of Albert Ellis. It merely reflects the fact we are most familiar with Beck's model and it is our principal aim to share with the reader the enthusiasm which we feel about recent developments in that tradition. We use the term 'therapy' to indicate the area of overlap between therapeutic counselling and psychotherapy. Throughout the book, we refer to the practitioners of cognitive therapy as both cognitive therapists and cognitive counsellors, in recognition that our readers may include both those who refer to themselves as cognitive therapists, and those who may refer to themselves as counsellors who practise cognitive therapy.

Acknowledgements

Diana and I both trained on the Oxford Certificate in Cognitive Therapy course, based at the Warneford Hospital in Oxford. The course was very thorough and inspiring. We would like to acknowledge the teaching staff of the course, especially Melanie Fennell, Ann Hackmann and Adrian Wells, who supervised our client work. The idea for this book first came to me during a workshop given at the invitation of Wyon Stansfeld, then of Employee Assistance Resources. The awkward questions posed that day and the answers we were able to move towards began to raise in me the hope that counsellors might be persuaded to give cognitive therapy a chance. My students and colleagues at University of Wales College Newport have continued to ask the awkward but useful questions that are essential to help one develop one's thinking. To all, my thanks – especially to Amelia Lyons, Anita Jaffe-Dick, Brian Hunter, Jean Bayliss and Annie Wills for reading drafts and making invaluable comments and suggestions. Throughout the writing, I've been sustained by the love and tolerance of my wife, Annie, and children, Joe and Laura. My father was very excited about me writing this but, unfortunately, did not live to see the final result. Finally, many thanks to my co-author, Diana, who graciously suggested that my name should be that of the first author. She has taught me what it means to be a serious author in this field. Although, we both wondered at times if the other would turn out to be 'The Co-Author from Hell', the end result, I believe, is far more like 'heaven on wheels'!

Frank Wills
February 1997

I would like to thank my colleagues at the Department of Psychology in Oxford, where I have learned cognitive therapy from many excellent teachers and supervisors over the years. I am grateful to Christine Küchemann and Tabitha Brufal for helpful comments on the manuscript. My husband, Mo Chandler, has been a source of continual support and encouragement, willing to be a Sage Widower, proof-reader and chef during my long periods of incarceration. The process of co-authoring the book has been exciting and challenging, and at times traumatic, and I am grateful to Frank for suggesting we write the book, and for keeping the wheels of progress firmly on the rails.

Diana Sanders
February 1997

Introduction: Transforming the Image of Cognitive Therapy

Cognitive therapy is, no doubt, a fast-growing and fashionable form of psychotherapy. It is widely used not only in the United States, where the therapy originally developed, but across the world. It is not uncommon for the founding father, Aaron T. Beck, to start his seminars on cognitive therapy by showing a map of the world, highlighting the spread of cognitive therapy centres. There appears to be a great demand for cognitive therapy, with increasing research on its applications to a wide range of emotional problems. Cognitive therapy has been more the realm of psychologists and psychiatrists than of counselling; however, the therapy is beginning to be taught on counselling courses, and a recent survey by the British Association of Counselling indicated that around one fifth of members defined their practice as cognitive counselling (Palmer and Szymonska, 1995).

Despite its popularity and development, the cognitive approach does not rest easily with the counselling world. For some years we have asked counselling trainees to describe their images of the different therapies and their respective therapists. The image attributed to cognitive therapy and cognitive therapists was remarkably consistent, revolving around the adjectives rational, cold, intellectual, analysing, clever and unemotional. Some even offered the image of Mr Spock from *Star Trek*. How did this rather unappealing and Vulcan image come about? One factor seems to be that the counselling world was until quite recently dominated by person-centred and psychodynamic models. The behavioural model was highly unattractive to counsellors because of its disdain of psychodynamic principles and because of its supposed 'mechanical' model of human nature, tending to make it, to paraphrase Oscar Wilde, 'the counselling model that dare not speak its name'. Another factor is the relative newness of the cognitive model. Albert Ellis did not fully develop rational-emotive behaviour therapy until the mid-1960s and Aaron T. Beck's work did not really gain wide currency until the late 1970s. Furthermore, these new therapies quickly claimed to be highly effective, at least within prescribed areas. For example, Beck's work on depression carried a well-developed research profile to back up its claims of effectiveness. Even when people were prepared to accept its effectiveness in the treatment of depression, there was scepticism with regard to the approach's effectiveness when applied to a wider range of problems. A critique of cognitive-behavioural approaches quickly developed around the following points:

1 Cognitive therapy was only useful in relatively prescribed areas such as depression.
2 Cognitive approaches downplayed or ignored emotions.
3 Cognitive approaches paid insufficient attention to 'real life' events and could be over-confrontational with and even detrimental to vulnerable clients.
4 Cognitive approaches did not take into account early experience and developmental issues.
5 Cognitive approaches downplayed or ignored the importance of the therapeutic relationship.

All these criticisms had and retain some force. The cognitive field, however, is a rapidly developing one and some of these points have already been successfully addressed. All of them are being worked with in significant ways. The problem for us as educators and trainers has been to keep minds open long enough to hear some of the more sophisticated nuances of the approach whilst, at the same time, teaching basic concepts from the early seminal works. As the literature on the whole field grows at an exponential rate, trainers are sometimes tempted to recycle somewhat out-of-date and simplistic versions of the theories of cognitive therapy, especially when the trainer is not enamoured with the approach.

This, however, leaves trainees with incomplete versions of the theory and practice of cognitive therapy, thereby perpetuating some of the myths outlined in Figure 1. We therefore begin our description of the cognitive approach to counselling with an up-to-date account of the model and practice of cognitive therapy as it has developed from Beck's original model, which goes a long way to answering these criticisms.

- Only the most intelligent patients will benefit.
- CT does not deal with feelings.
- CT does not look at important past events/childhood experience.
- CT does not use/look at the therapeutic relationship.
- CT is not suitable for people with long-term difficulties/personality disorders.
- CT aims to get people to accept difficult life circumstances by the 'power of positive thinking'.

Figure 1   *Myths about cognitive therapy*

Criticisms and Answers

The therapeutic model presented in *Cognitive Therapy of Depression* (Beck et al., 1979) has become the most identified description of what people know about cognitive therapy and was certainly a key milestone in the development of the therapy. However, the fact that this book developed from a deliberately prescriptive manual used for research protocols may have resulted in some people who have just read this one book concluding that cognitive therapy is mechanical in its approach. Further, the lack of focus on the therapeutic relationship, on concepts such as transference and countertransference, and the focus on particular problems possibly at the expense of others, led to critical debates and perhaps started cognitive therapy's negative reputation in the counselling world. The more recent history of cognitive therapy, however, represents several key developments in five main areas.

1. Widening the Field of Cognitive Therapy
The cognitive model has been elaborated to cover areas other than depression. Beck et al. (1985) have written on anxiety; Beck has focused on cognitive therapy for couples, in his publication *Love is Never Enough* (Beck, 1988), and, with colleagues, has expanded the cognitive approach to long-term therapy, focusing on underlying schemata, in *Cognitive Therapy of Personality Disorders* (Beck et al., 1990). Beck has also developed cognitive approaches to suicide, inpatient treatments and drug abuse, which remain his current interests. A growing army of researchers and writers have developed the model in other areas, including therapy for panic

(Clark, 1986), generalised anxiety disorder (Butler et al., 1991), obsessive-compulsive disorder (Salkovskis and Kirk, 1989), social phobia (Wells, 1995), substance abuse (Beck et al., 1993), inpatient treatment of depression (Wright et al., 1993), health anxiety (Salkovskis, 1989), psychosomatic problems (Sanders, 1996) and eating disorders (Fairburn and Cooper, 1989), to name but a few. As cognitive therapy has broadened to become an effective treatment for people with emotional difficulties, psychological problems and personality problems, important advances in both theory and practice have been made (Clark and Fairburn, 1996). In particular, the extension into a wide range of emotional disorders has led to a growing interest in the way clients can be helped to understand more about how they attribute meaning to physical and psychological experiences of self. For example, it appears that panic sufferers attribute catastrophic interpretations to relatively normal bodily symptoms (Clark, 1986); people who are socially phobic exaggerate the way they perceive others' perceptions of them, based on internal rather than external cues (Clark and Wells, 1995); and people with obsessional and compulsive disorders interpret their own thoughts as evidence that they are bad people or responsible for bad things happening (Salkovskis, 1985).

2. Emotion and Cognitive Therapy

Emotion has been accorded a much more significant role in cognitive approaches. Although some of the earlier models may have given the message that emotions are linked to 'irrational' beliefs, Beck (1976) makes it clear that the relevant appraisals are not so much irrational as exaggerated and not supported by objective evidence. In his later publications (Beck et al., 1985, 1990) Beck and his colleagues advance evidence that exaggerated appraisals may even have evolutionary survival value: depression may be a biologically wired-in response to disappointment, acting as a conserving mechanism and protecting the individual from disappointment (Beck, 1987); anxiety enables humans to react rapidly to danger; and specific phobias may protect us from specific dangers. Some other research has even suggested that a degree of slightly positive exaggeration may be associated with positive mental health (Taylor, 1983). Publications by both Beck and his colleagues (Beck et al., 1985) and others (Safran and Greenberg, 1988) make it clear that the relationship between cognition and emotion is highly complex. Whatever very sophisticated psychological model we may eventually build to link cognition and emotion, it will often be the client's experience that the emotion seems to come first or at least simultaneously with the cognitive appraisal. Cognitive therapists need to be thoroughly at home working with emotions, for, as Beck has frequently pointed out, 'If you're not working with the emotion, you're not where the action is' (Beck, 1994). The client's emotional response, rather than being seen as a problem, can be seen as providing vital information about his experience, and rather than coming to him via cognition, the emotion itself can be seen as a vital response to events in the world. The emotion contains crucial cognitive elements, providing a therapist with a point of leverage into the whole client experience.

3. The Role of the External World

Newer advances in cognitive therapy have clarified that although cognitive therapy focuses much of its effort on internal cognitive processes, it is not downplaying the role of external events and processes. It is easy to offend clients by seeming to imply that their problems are all due to 'distorted' beliefs and are therefore not 'real' problems. One of the key criticisms of early cognitive approaches was the lack of discussion of the role of relationships and the influence of external environment in human emotion and emotional difficulties (Coyne and Gotlib, 1983). Beck's early models of depression focused on individual characteristics; later formulations included the interaction between individual characteristics and life events, in particular the social environment. His reformulation of depression included the notion that specific external events impact on different people in different ways depending on the individual's specific cognitive vulnerabilities to depression. In particular, Beck (1983, 1987) hypothesised an interaction between types of personality and types of stressful life events. He conceptualised two broad modes of personality: sociotropy, characterised by a need for positive social interaction; and autonomy, characterised by a need for achievement, freedom from control from others, and a need for solitude. Sociotropic individuals were found to become depressed following a disruption of social bonding; autonomous individuals, when they were unable to achieve goals. Cognitive theorists and therapists are now paying increasing attention to the interpersonal side of both clients' lives and therapy itself (Safran and Segal, 1990), using cognitive analysis to look at how various rules of relationships have been learned and operationalised.

4. *Personality Issues and Long-Term Therapy*

Cognitive therapy has paid increasing attention to clients' underlying personality patterns, often related to early experience. This has become necessary because of the finding that standard cognitive therapy is less effective when clients do have underlying personality issues (Van Nelzen and Emmelkamp, 1996), particularly when offering cognitive therapy for depression (Scott et al., 1995). Clients with long-standing difficulties, particularly when they have had traumatic early experiences, may find it helpful to learn to monitor and evaluate their thinking, problem-solve, and try to work out alternative ways of viewing situations or behaving. However, their basic beliefs about themselves may always get in the way and leave the individual at risk of relapse. Further, clients with personality disorders are more likely to drop out of standard therapy, thus compromising its effectiveness (Van Nelzen and Emmelkamp, 1996). In particular, Young (1994) examines how some of the assumptions of standard cognitive therapy – that clients have access to their feelings, thoughts and images; that they have specific difficulties on which to focus; and that they are able to engage with the counsellor and form a therapeutic relationship within a few sessions – do not hold true for clients with personality disorders, thus necessitating adaptations of the approach. Therefore, identifying and working with these basic beliefs, and adapting the form of therapy, becomes crucial. Several different strands are evident in cognitive therapy's development into the field of personality change: Beck et al.'s (1990) work with 'personality disorders', Young's (1994) work on 'schema-focused' cognitive therapy and Mary Ann Layden et al.'s (1993) work on 'borderline' personalities. These points will be explored in Chapter 6.

5. *The Therapeutic Relationship*

In recognising the need to adapt cognitive therapy for work with deeper issues, a vital element has been the development of a fuller understanding of the therapeutic relationship. In the original model, the therapeutic relationship was defined as one of 'collaborative empiricism'. This was conceptualised as one which used many of the Rogerian concepts such as warmth and empathic understanding but mainly in order to establish a working relationship. The relationship was seen as a base from which to do the cognitive work and not as an end in itself. However, there is increasing recognition of the need to identify and work with the client's characteristic 'interpersonal pull' (Safran and Segal, 1990) and countertransference (Layden et al., 1993), especially with clients with underlying personality issues. The therapeutic relationship in cognitive therapy is the major focus of Chapters 3 and 6; working with difficulties in the therapeutic relationship is discussed in Chapter 7.

Conclusion

Having given this brief introduction to the development of cognitive therapy and some of its newer aspects, we have aimed to give the reader hope that some of the cruder criticisms of cognitive therapy may be unfounded. In the succeeding chapters, we aim to bring together the newer strands of theory and practice that have been developing, and make them user-friendly and accessible to counsellors. More ambitiously, we hope that we have been able to inspire the reader to regard, at least as a testable hypothesis, our belief that cognitive therapy is a comprehensive approach using an exciting cornucopia of imaginative and effective techniques, integrated into an overall conceptual model, for helping counsellors deal with most of the clients who will come their way. We hope that the reader will allow us to demonstrate that we have also taken good note of Paul Gilbert's entreaty that cognitive therapists should 'take more time out of their technique-oriented approaches and consider what it is to be a human being' (in Dryden and Trower, 1988, p. 66).

PART I
A COGNITIVE MODEL FOR COUNSELLORS USING THE CASE CONCEPTUALISATION APPROACH

1

The Original Model and its Recent Developments

Clients very rarely come into therapy asking for help with their negative thoughts. They come to therapy because they are feeling bad. Despite its focus on thinking, cognitive therapy is actually all about reaching and working with clients' salient feelings. Cognitions are emphasised because they can often provide the most direct and useful path to emotions, and the easiest way to access the key and 'hot' emotions connected to the client's difficulties. Further, clients' specific cognitions and style of thinking can go a long way to explain their feelings, thus making the often incomprehensible degree of emotion more understandable to them. With his two major publications of the 1970s, *Cognitive Therapy and the Emotional Disorders* (Beck, 1976), and *Cognitive Therapy of Depression* (Beck et al., 1979), Beck and his colleagues laid down what many now regard as the original model of cognitive therapy. The model contained a theory of how people became emotionally disturbed, a model of how they could alleviate and eliminate disturbance, and a model of how further disturbance might be prevented. An original feature of the model was the idea of 'cognitive specificity', which showed how different types of disturbance had different cognitive roots. The links between emotion and cognition were initially most clearly demonstrated and developed in the treatment of depression, opportunely because depression is often regarded as one of the most frequently presenting problems (Fennell, 1989). The model was also backed up with what was, for the psychotherapy field, an impressive range of research validation in terms of both process and outcome. This chapter describes these aspects of the original model of emotional disturbance and therapy process, and then goes on to describe the extension and developments of the 1980s and 1990s.

The Original Model of Emotional Disturbance

The Thought–Emotion Cycle

One of the aims in cognitive therapy is to look at the meaning the client is giving to situations, emotions or biology, expressed as the client's 'negative automatic thoughts'. The valuable concept of cognitive specificity demonstrates the linking of particular types of appraising thoughts to particular emotions and the influence that they have over our behaviour, as shown in Figure 1.1. The appraisal 'danger', for example, raises anxiety and primes us for evasive, defensive or other reaction. The appraisal of 'loss' to our domain is likely to invoke sadness and mourning behaviour. The appraisal of 'unfair' is likely to arouse anger and a possible 'fight' response.

In themselves, the responses to our appraisals are not necessarily problematic and are often functional: for example, we all know that driving carries certain risks; thinking about the risks may, hopefully, make us better drivers. However, our specific appraisals of events, both internal and external, begin to be more problematic as the appraisals themselves become more exaggerated. If we start to become preoccupied with the risks of

Appraisal	Emotion
Loss to domain	Sadness, Depression
Threat to domain	Fear, Anxiety
Violation of domain	Anger
Expansion to domain	Delight

Figure 1.1   *Key themes: cognitive specificity*

driving, and begin to see ourselves having an accident, then our emotion of slight, functional anxiety becomes one of unease or even panic. Furthermore, if this feeling increases, the chances of our driving ability being adversely affected also increase. Similarly, we may feel a certain comforting sadness about a loss in our life, but if we begin to see the loss as being a major erosion of our being, we begin to feel corrosive depression rather than relatively soulful melancholy. If the depression cycle goes on, we tend to become lifeless, lacking energy and enthusiasm, and are thereby less likely to engage in the things that give our life meaning; as a result we become even more depressed. The essence of the model is that emotional difficulties begin when the way we see events gets exaggerated beyond the available evidence; these exaggerated ways of seeing things tend to have negative influences on our feelings and behaviour, in a vicious cycle.

Cognitive therapy is often wrongly held to be based on the generalised formula that people are disturbed by their thoughts. In fact, a good cognitive therapist would try to understand the client in a highly individualised way. Rather than reducing a client's mediating cognitions to a formulaic set of 'irrational beliefs', the cognitive approach aims to understand why the client is appraising events in particular ways and why she feels the way that she does. An external event will have a very different impact on different people because each individual has, firstly, a different personal domain (that is, of cherished values, interests or possessions) on which the events impinge; and, secondly, an idiosyncratic way of appraising the event because cognitions, perceptions, beliefs and schemata will have been shaped by the individual's unique personal experiences and life history. The aim of cognitive therapy is to understand both the person's personal domain and his idiosyncratic way of appraising events. Whilst, on a simplistic level, a person's thoughts and emotions about an event may appear 'irrational', given his way of seeing the world, the response may be entirely rational.

Cognitive Distortions: Negative Thoughts

Cognitive themes are expressed in specific thoughts. We think only rarely in themes themselves, such as 'There is a loss to my personal domain'. More often we think in specific cognitions which, when added together, amount to a theme. These themes become elaborated and maintained by the day-to-day 'dripping tap' effect of the client's 'negative automatic thoughts' (NATs).

Often the client is barely aware of these thoughts until the counsellor highlights their existence. In depression, thinking has a characteristically negative tone centred on loss – not just of loved objects but of a sense of self-esteem and, crucially, for depression, a sense of loss of hopefulness about the world and the future. The triangle of negative view of self, negative view of the world and negative view of the future comprise Beck's famous 'cognitive triad', in which the dynamics of depression operate (Beck, 1967). Beck first discovered this continual negative commentary when a client became anxious whilst talking about past sexual experiences but revealed to him that it was the thought that Beck would think the client 'boring' rather than telling of the experiences that was causing the emotional pain (Beck, 1976).

In his 1976 book, Beck describes a range of cognitive distortions, shown in Figure 1.2. For example, the thought 'I'm stupid', a very common negative automatic thought in emotional disturbance, betrays 'all-or-nothing' thinking because it usually actually means that because I do some 'stupid' things, this makes me stupid. There appear to be only two possible conditions – doing everything right and being 'not stupid' or doing some things wrong and being 'stupid'. Thus the negatively biased person begins to self-blame, thereby depressing mood even further in the vicious cycle described below.

Identifying and labelling negative thoughts and seeing how emotions and thoughts interact in a vicious cycle are the first steps towards enabling the client to understand her emotions. When a client detects specific thoughts, it can be useful to ask her what effect that repetitive thought will have on her mood. Many will conclude that such thinking is bound to get them down. Thus the simplest form of the cognitive model (Figure 1.3) links the thoughts and emotions which are most relevant to the client's situation.

From Thoughts to Schemata

Negative automatic thoughts are those cognitions which are closest to the surface of consciousness. Beck recognised, however, that there were also deeper cognitions which incline the person to interpret events in relatively fixed patterns. Working in parallel with personal construct theorists (Kelly, 1955), he began to conceptualise the idea of cognitive structures. Beck initially used, and then abandoned, Kelly's term 'constructs', preferring the descriptions of earlier psychologists, such as Bartlett (1932), by using the

All-or-nothing thinking: Polarisation into two extreme categories of a phenomenon which really exists on a continuum. For example: 'safe' is when there is no risk at all; 'danger' when there is a slight risk; being OK is when I make no mistakes at all; being bad is when I make even a small mistake.

Mental filter: Positive information is excluded, leaving the field dominated by negative information. For example, concluding 'I never get things right' after making one small mistake, despite numerous life achievements.

Over-generalisation: Taking one negative event and using it to conclude that everything is going wrong. For example: spilling a cup of coffee at breakfast and concluding 'Everything is going wrong today'.

Jumping to conclusions: Going straight to a negative interpretation when there is little or no evidence to support this. For example: you end up by yourself at break-time and conclude, 'My colleagues are avoiding me'.

Discounting the positive: Positive experiences are dismissed on grounds such as, 'Anyone could have done that'.

Magnification: Difficulties and shortcomings are exaggerated. For example, forgetting a name and concluding 'I'm useless at relationships'.

'Should' statements: Tyrannical demands that oneself, others or the world in general *must* be some other way than they actually are.

Emotional reasoning: The assumption that negative emotions are a completely accurate guide to reality – 'I just feel they all hate me therefore they do all hate me'.

Labelling: The attachment of a personality 'tag' to a piece of behaviour. For example: failing at a job interview means 'I'm a failure'.

Personalisation: Holding oneself responsible for an event outside one's control. For example: 'My husband wouldn't drink if I was a beter wife'.

Mind reading: Guessing the content of someone else's thoughts, without checking it out with them: 'You're just saying that to be nice'; 'She thought I was terrible'.

Crystal ball gazing: Predicting the future: 'It's bad now so it will always be awful'; 'I'm going to make a complete fool of myself'.

Figure 1.2   *Cognitive distortions leading to disturbance (Burns, 1980; Fennell, 1989)*

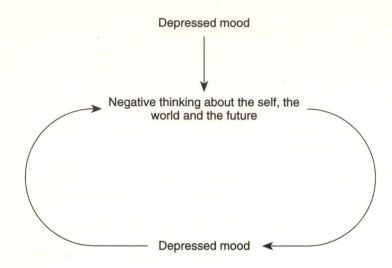

Figure 1.3   *Vicious cycle: simple form*

term 'schema' or the plural form 'schemata' to describe cognitive structures. Schemata are not, of course, all problematic. For example, following the work of John Bowlby, it appears that children who have experienced satisfactory bonding to primary care-givers will develop a basic set of rules or schemata which contain the inner working model that 'people can generally be trusted' (Bowlby, 1969). If a person who has this kind of 'trust' schema meets untrustworthy behaviour in another, he is likely to think, 'Something went wrong there, I may have to be more cautious in future', which is an adaptive response. In the opposite case, where a person with a 'mistrust' schema encounters untrustworthy behaviour, she is likely to conclude, 'I was right – you can't trust anyone – I won't do so again', which is an over-generalised and, therefore, maladaptive response. In the original cognitive model, negative schemata were seen as having an underlying relationship to NATs. The assumptions contained in schemata are triggered by events and lead to NATs. Sometimes the assumptions persisted after the NATs and symptoms of depression had cleared up. The assumptions may then be targeted as a method of preventing later relapse into depression. In the newer model, schemata are given a more significant and autonomous role in therapy.

The Role of Behaviour in Disturbance

So far we have established that there is a strong link between thought and feeling. We do not, as Beck did not, argue that this is a causal link. The link is best understood, and is likely to be experienced as such by the client, as a two-way process. Thoughts and feelings are experienced as unitary and it is likely that our labelling of 'thought' and 'feeling' is more a useful therapeutic device than a knowable reality. A similar line of reasoning is best applied to fitting behaviour into the picture. Again, the behaviour may be experienced as almost instantaneous – 'I couldn't help blurting it out'. Often, it will be helpful to the client to start to be aware of the accompanying thoughts and feelings that go with the behaviour, enabling him to make the response less automatic and therefore less problematic. The behavioural response often seems to play the final link in the chain, locking the whole sequence of thought–feeling–behaviour into the 'neurotic paradox' – the tendency of dysfunctional patterns to maintain themselves.

Examples of linking thoughts, behaviour and disturbance are given below.

> Keith is aged 40. He is a computer project manager in the Civil Service and has experienced recurrent depression since his teenage years. His current depression has lasted for two years, since the prospect of his work section being privatised. He is somewhat isolated at work, works hard, stays late and takes work home. He also considered that his performance was deteriorating, thus making him even more vulnerable to redundancy. Keith's pattern is shown in Figure 1.4.

Figure 1.4   *Keith's vicious cycle*

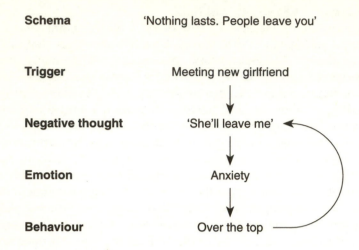

Schema   'Nothing lasts. People leave you'

Trigger   Meeting new girlfriend

Negative thought   'She'll leave me'

Emotion   Anxiety

Behaviour   Over the top

Figure 1.5   *Ben's vicious cycle*

Ben had lost his mother 10 years previously. He came to believe 'Nothing lasts. People leave you'. When he meets a possible girlfriend, he feels very anxious because he imagines her leaving him. He then tends to become 'over the top' in the relationship, thus making it more likely that the relationship will not last. Ben's cycle is as shown in Figure 1.5.

Clients are often puzzled by their emotional and behavioural reactions to situations – 'I can't understand why I get drawn into doing that' being a common response. For the therapist and client to actually draw the 'vicious cycle' onto a piece of paper can make the whole cycle seem more concrete and understandable – and *ipso facto* more likely to be open to change. The diagram may be given to clients as something to take home and think about or work on – perhaps as part of a homework assignment. The process of case conceptualisation is described in detail in Chapter 2.

The Original Model of the Therapy Process

Cognitive therapy aims to be an accessible, common-sense and practical mode of therapy. One of its attractions is its immediacy, fitting with the client's experience, and appearing to students of its approach as simple and straightforward. Although such associations belie the complexities and sophistication of the cognitive model and cognitive therapy, its congruence with our and our client's experience enables the therapy to make sense and, therefore, fit the facts.

The process of cognitive therapy specified in the early models, which has been strongly continued in recent developments, involved three elements: a collaborative therapeutic relationship; a scientific, empirical method; and a parsimonious form of therapy. In Chapter 3 of *Cognitive Therapy of Depression*, Beck et al. (1979) describe a view of the *therapeutic relationship* which draws heavily on the work of Carl Rogers, stressing the 'core conditions' of 'warmth, accurate empathy and genuineness' (p. 45). They add, however, that these conditions are not in themselves sufficient to produce optimum therapeutic effect. In addition to these conditions, the authors also describe trust, rapport and collaboration. It is this last concept and the related idea of collaborative empiricism which mark the point of departure from Rogers:

> In contrast to 'supportive' or 'relationship' therapy, the therapeutic relationship is not used simply as the instrument to alleviate suffering but as a vehicle to facilitate a common effort in carrying out specific goals. In this sense, the therapist and the [client] form a 'team'. (Beck et al., 1979, p. 54)

The emphasis here is on a working relationship: one that perhaps carries with it a little of the Protestant work ethic, offering a contrast to other therapies which stress the importance of 'being' rather than 'doing' in the relationship with the client. The nature of the work to be carried out is that of identifying maladaptive cognitive processes and challenging or modifying them.

A second aspect of the therapy process is that cognitive therapy is a *scientific* and empirical form of therapy. The matter is first investigated and therapy proceeds from the findings of this assessment. As will be discussed in greater detail in Chapter 4, assessment involves full understanding of the presenting symptoms and underlying factors, allowing a clear direction for the therapy and establishment of a base-line from which the comparative outcome of the therapy can be measured. Measures such as the BDI (Beck Depression Inventory) and the BAI (Beck Anxiety Inventory) are used to assess both base-line and progress during therapy. By the time the allocated 12–20 sessions (for depression, 5–20 for anxiety) are coming to an end, the scores should be considerably reduced. Thus therapeutic interventions can be regarded as a series of scientific experiments to be judged on their results. The degree of symptom relief would be one factor in determining whether the therapy can really end as planned. Further, cognitive therapy seeks to elicit feedback from the client: both during and at the end of each therapy session, to enable client and therapist to evaluate the interventions and progress. A final aspect of the scientific approach is the standardisation of the way the therapy is conducted, delineated in rating scales such as the Cognitive Therapy Scale (Young and Beck, 1980; reproduced in Freeman et al., 1990). In this way, the characteristic and effective ingredients of the therapy aim to meet criteria which are consistent across therapy as well as therapists.

Thirdly, the *parsimony* of cognitive therapy is achieved by starting work at the symptom level and only going on to work at the underlying level when it becomes necessary either from the way therapy unfolds or from the need to militate against later relapse after a relatively successful therapy. For example, the cognitive therapy of depression often starts at the behavioural level, moving to working on cognitions and underlying assumptions only when behavioural approaches have produced some improvement in mood (Fennell, 1989). In depression, behavioural withdrawal is a profound feature and one which has a powerfully reinforcing effect on maintaining low mood. The client would be often encouraged to schedule activities and then try to insert more 'mastery' and 'pleasure' activities into the day – the draining of pleasure from the client's life is again a powerful factor which reinforces the depression. The aim of using these behavioural tasks is to promote the overall therapeutic goal of loosening the grip of depressogenic thinking on the client's mood and functioning. Thus, a pleasurable activity can be used to test and, hopefully, disconfirm the client's negative automatic thought 'I never enjoy things any more'. As the client's mood lifts, it should be possible to do more and more directly cognitive work. Again the parsimonious approach is evident in that it is usually recommended that one starts to work at the shallowest level of cognition – that of the automatic thought – and only later works at the deeper assumption and schema levels. The great array of both behavioural and cognitive techniques gives much flexibility to 'mix and match' the therapeutic intervention. Good cognitive therapy should, however, always be carefully fitted to the individual client. Although the standard formula for a depressed client may be to move from behaviour to cognition to assumption, the therapy process needs to be modified as appropriate.

Clients who did not respond to standard models and processes tended to be described as presenting 'technical problems' for cognitive therapy. Amongst the responses to such clients would be adjustments to therapeutic procedures and perhaps different treatment mixes, including drug and group therapy. It has only been in more recent years that it began to be seen that some clients might benefit from a completely different type of cognitive therapy. These newer models of psychological disturbance and the process of cognitive therapy are described next.

The Newer Model of Psychological Disturbance

Since the development of the original cognitive model of psychological disturbance, a number of new ways of thinking about psychological disturbance have been integrated into the cognitive model. Three areas are discussed below: (a) integrating the interpersonal perspective and the development of cognitive interpersonal styles into the model; (b) integrating the meaning of somatic symptoms into cognitive models; and (c) an interest in meta-cognition: thinking about thinking.

Interpersonal Processes and the Cognitive Model

Safran and Segal (1990) add strength and depth to traditional cognitive therapy by building in a clearer understanding of the client's relationship issues outside the therapy and emphasising the interpersonal aspects of the therapeutic relationship itself. As other therapies have long emphasised, there is often a strong relationship between the interpersonal factors outside the therapy situation and those within (Strupp and Binder, 1984). Safran and Segal, following on the earlier work of Guidano and Liotti (1983), integrate such interpersonal issues into the context of a perspective which owes much to John Bowlby, especially his concept of attachment, focusing on the strong imperative for humans to relate to others. Relatedness has crucial survival value not only to the infant during the long period of dependency but also to all of us, as our lives are usually dependent on large degrees of social co-operation. Attachment behaviour is seen as a 'wired-in' propensity of human behaviour. Attachment seeking behaviour is evident right from the first moments of a newborn baby's experiences. This view is backed by a mass of evidence from developmental studies (for example, Ainsworth, 1982; Bowlby, 1969, 1973, 1980; Sroufe, 1979; Stern, 1985). For example, infants seem to quickly develop the ability to send attachment messages to and receive messages from the care-giver. Misattunements in sending or receiving information, if consistent, can at this stage have a highly negative effect on development.

As a result of our imperative to relate, many of the key core beliefs and assumptions that we hold about life and the world are likely to be interpersonal. Attachment schemata are internalised and become very persistent, somewhat independently of subsequent experience. They can therefore become locked into, in Safran and Segal's terms, a cognitive-interpersonal style. The process is illustrated with Jane.

> Jane remembered her childhood as one in which she did not get recognition and considered that she did not 'measure up' to her siblings in her parents' eyes. Consequently, a strong desire to please others developed during her childhood. Forty years later, she could not understand why her colleagues at work didn't respect her. Her tactic was to try very hard to please them – to win their respect. Unfortunately, as often happens with this tactic, it made her colleagues even more irritated and less respectful to her.

In practice, clients often seem to bring the types of interpersonal difficulties described by Jane into therapy. As Harry Stack Sullivan (1953) points out, the client's attempted solution is often part of the problem, that is, the client, understandably, tries to counter the dysfunctional belief, yet in a way that only leads to its perpetuation. Part of the therapist's assessment of the client is to see how pervasive and enduring these patterns are. We would frequently expect to see them replayed within the therapeutic relationship itself. Safran and Segal (1990) suggest that therapists need to be aware of 'interpersonal markers', not only because such awareness is likely to facilitate the therapeutic process but also because they can prove to be 'windows into the client's whole cognitive-interpersonal style' (p. 82). We turn again to Jane.

> The first time that I (FW) met Jane, she asked me a lot about my qualifications as a therapist. I initially made what I guess is the standard interpretation of her actions – that they might conceal an anxiety about trust. In a later discussion, however, she linked her inquiries with her cognitive-interpersonal belief that: 'People will only be interested in me if I am very interested in them first'. She had actually been taught a form of this belief as part of training in sales. A look back at the previous extract on her will, however, show how well this belief fitted into her existing cognitive-interpersonal schema, 'I am only able to gain love and respect by pleasing people'.

Safran and Segal (1990) also link this interpersonal focus with the work of Greenberg and Safran (1984, 1987) on emotion in cognitive therapy. This work criticised earlier models of cognitive therapy as being overly rationalistic and utilitarian in their approach to emotions. Sometimes painful emotions have been seen as needing to be brought under control. There has, however, been a growing realisation in most forms of cognitive therapy that, as Beck has long said, emotion is the key to successful therapy. The need for emotional salience has to be particularly understood in relation to interpersonal schemata. These schemata are likely to be encoded in highly emotional ways, so unless the therapeutic process activates at least some of this emotion, processing their meaning is unlikely to have much therapeutic impact. As indicated earlier, the relevant interpersonal beliefs may have been established in the client's earliest days and therefore much of the influential encoding will have been done in non-verbal ways, which means in turn that such encoding and meanings may not be touched by directly verbal interventions. This again highlights the role of the therapeutic relationship, especially as a forum within which 'interpersonal markers', which can be regarded as a sample of the client's interpersonal schemata, can be contained, explored and worked through.

The recognition of the importance of interpersonal schemata and the therapeutic relationship began to transform the picture of cognitive therapy. It moved from a therapy in which the therapist could appear as the stereotyped cool, detached logic-chopping technician, to a therapy in which 'emotion-and-thinking-and-behaving' is the central concern; and in which the therapist has to have a crucially here-and-now awareness of how the triad is played out in the therapeutic relationship itself, as well as in the client's life outside therapy. This awareness demands a high degree of self-knowledge – an awareness emphasised more readily in other therapies but now a necessary part of cognitive therapy. In many ways, however, this leaves the original structure of cognitive therapy much as it was. The difference lies in the quality of what goes on inside the structure. The structure only really changes when the therapist decides that the client's difficulties are such that a 'holding relationship' (Winnicott, 1965) may be necessary. In this case, the active, directive phase of the original cognitive therapy model is postponed until a considerable period has been spent on building up the therapeutic relationship. Even then, the actual active cognitive therapy stage will be crucially directed at underlying assumptions and schemata. Although this model is still very much developing, the clearest accounts of it are emerging as 'schema-focused cognitive therapy' (Beck et al., 1990; Layden et al., 1993; Young, 1994).

Cognition and Physiology

Physiology has always played an important part in the cognitive model, particularly in the understanding of anxiety (Beck et al., 1985). Recent models of anxiety have looked in greater detail at the way people interpret bodily cues (interoception), which has been shown to play a key role in panic attacks (Clark, 1986). It has been shown that people prone to panic attacks tend to make catastrophic interpretations of relatively normal bodily symptoms. They are often prevented from learning that these symptoms are normal and relatively benign by the use of 'safety behaviours' (Salkovskis, 1991; Salkovskis et al., 1996). The following examples illustrate how new thinking about physical symptoms may be integrated into the cognitive model.

> Kevin is a student nurse, prone to panic attacks. When he feels his pulse suddenly racing, he feels as if he is going to collapse, and therefore be seen as unable to do his job. The catastrophic thoughts lead to a growing sense of panic, with increasing physical symptoms to match. He then uses a safety behaviour – he sits down. After a worrisome half-hour, the symptoms begin to sub-side. Because he has not collapsed, he deduces that sitting down has saved him. He is not able to learn that he probably never would have collapsed, and even if he had, it is unlikely to have led to the catastrophe he feared. His panic-inducing belief therefore remains intact and able to strike again another day.

The role of physiology is also important in conceptualising depression, as the following example illustrates.

> Jim reported that every morning he awoke feeling physically uncomfortable, stiff and 'down'. He habitually thought, 'Oh no, not another day feeling like shit'. When he was able to step back and monitor this feeling more closely, he realised that he often felt some bladder and bowel discomfort because he wanted to go to the toilet. When he simply went to the toilet and set about getting ready for the day, he noticed that he felt much less uncomfortable and 'down'. He was then able to resist making negative predictions about the rest of the day. He also discussed his physical sensations on waking with his wife. Although she did not get such symptoms, she reported feeling very tired in the early evening. As Jim felt better in the evening, he was able to redefine himself as 'different from' rather than 'inferior to' his wife. These two pieces of learning

were a significant part of his successful attempts to get out of the vicious cycle of depression.

Meta-Cognition

Traditionally, cognitive therapy has tended to work with the language (declarative) content of negative thoughts and beliefs. When new therapists first try cognitive methods, they often report the difficulty that the client may be intellectually convinced that they are not 'stupid', yet it may continue to 'feel as if' they are. This may be because traditional cognitive methods which challenge the content of thought are only challenging the output of the relevant cognitive processes whereas they would be more effective if they addressed the processes themselves – that is, explored how people arrive at what they 'know'.

The concepts of meta-cognition include an analysis of how individuals' thinking about their thinking plays a key role in disturbance. For example, the client who is anxious about everything has numerous negative, anxious thoughts. What is of interest is not simply the content and meaning of specific thoughts, but the meaning of thinking in this particular way. Wells and Matthews (1994) distinguish between direct (type 1) worries and these meta-cognitive (type 2) worries. Wells (1994, 1995, 1996), Clark and Wells (1995) and Wells and Butler (1996) show the importance of meta-cognition (thinking about thinking) in the problems of both general anxiety and social phobia. They show how beliefs such as 'Worrying keeps me protected from nasty surprises' reinforce the problem and incubate further difficulty. The process is illustrated by Sasha, a 43-year-old insurance clerk.

Sasha worried about everything. She woke up worrying about the day, and went to bed worrying about what had happened in the day and what might happen the next day. She worried about her husband, her daughter, her health and world affairs. Therapy initially focused on the content of these worries, her cognitive distortions, and learning to spot and challenge her thinking. She reported that the process of evaluating her thoughts made sense in her head, but she continued to feel awful, worrying as much as before. The therapy then moved to a meta-cognitive level, looking at the meaning of her worrying thoughts. She believed that not worrying would mean the things that she worried about were more likely to happen; worrying somehow alerted her to the possibility of danger, so she could act more quickly, and indeed prevented terrible things happening in the first place. If she did not worry, she might forget to do things. Therefore, stepping outside her thought content to look at the meaning of the process was necessary before Sasha could begin to change her worry patterns.

Salkovskis offers a similar analysis for people with obsessive-compulsive difficulties, where the client believes that the fact she is having bad thoughts in itself proves something bad about her. Bad thoughts may also be taken as an indication that something bad might happen, indicating a sense of the client's excessive degree of personal responsibility for harm to self or others (Salkovskis, 1985; Salkovskis and Kirk, 1989; Salkovskis et al., 1995). To try to deal with their thoughts, these clients often combine ritualistic behaviours, such as compulsive washing or checking, with 'neutralising', such as trying to stop the thoughts or replace them with 'good' thoughts. As a result they are prevented from learning that the thoughts are normal and harmless. Therefore, as well as working on the specific content of the thoughts, analysis of the meaning of the thought processes is a more effective and fruitful intervention. For example, Christopher felt plagued with anxiety after walking past someone in the street and imagining them slipping on the wet pavement and hurting themselves. He felt extremely guilty, believing that the fact he had those thoughts was as good as him wanting the accident to happen, and may even increase the likelihood of an accident for which he would be responsible. If someone was to slip and hurt themselves, he would not only be responsible for injury to another person, but doubly responsible because he had the chance to prevent catastrophe but did nothing about it. He attempted to assuage his guilt by praying, several times an hour.

The Newer Model of the Therapy Process

The scope of cognitive therapy is widening – both in terms of its application to an increasing number of difficulties and in terms of a wider use of therapeutic interventions within its overall structure. In this new scenario, the concept of formulation or conceptualisation, described in detail in Chapter 2, becomes ever more useful. If we think of the conceptualisation as a kind of map of the client issues that are likely to be relevant to therapy, then we can see that it offers us many different points at which we may start and many different possible directions in which we may proceed. We could, for example, choose to proceed in the way of orthodox cognitive work and begin to work at the symptom level

- the 'bottom-up' approach. The new emphasis in cognitive therapy on working with emotions allows us to work in a primary way on the feeling level, perhaps taking techniques from the experiential therapies, such as Gestalt (J. Beck, 1995; Edwards, 1989). There is also a growing interest on working with emotions and imagery within a cognitive framework (J. Beck, 1995; Edwards, 1989, 1990; Layden et al., 1993; Wells and Hackmann, 1993). Wells and Hackmann (1993), for example, show that clients' negative images in health anxiety, such as images of coffins, death or permanent disability, play a strong role in maintaining anxious symptoms, and that these negative images can be greatly attenuated as part of both symptom relief and general therapeutic change. Interestingly, working with imagery was advocated early on by Beck (1970a), yet this seems to have been, until recently, a neglected clarion call. Beck's initial interest was in using imagery as a way of understanding the meaning that the client attributes to images or dreams. Emery, in a later work on anxiety (Beck et al., 1985), pointed out, however, that merely repeating the image several times often resulted in the development of a more functional imagery. Influenced by Gestalt therapy, more recent cognitive approaches have shown a greater capacity to experiment with transforming imagery.

As new ways of working in cognitive therapy evolve, rather than starting at the level of thoughts, there is always the option of 'top-down' work, working with deeper level of cognitions – assumptions, core beliefs and schemata. Such levels can be deeper and less conscious than the more surface level of negative thoughts; therefore this style of therapy may bear some resemblance to psychodynamic therapy. The more explorative style of the 'constructivist' approach advocated by Guidano and Liotti (1983; Guidano, 1991; Liotti, 1987, 1991), for example, lays more stress on taking a developmental history and on spending more time working at that level. Assessment in cognitive therapy now includes more of a historical and developmental analysis, allowing for more of an understanding of the origins of the client's core beliefs; and also allowing for the need of many of our clients at the beginning of therapy to tell their stories from the beginning, giving a top-down historical perspective on their difficulties.

In the newer models of the therapy process, events in the therapeutic relationship can be used as markers, for both client and therapist, of dysfunctional patterns of relating which are repeated outside of therapy. Safran and Segal (1990) have borrowed many ideas from both experiential and psychodynamic therapy to build a cognitive-interpersonal style for working with the therapeutic relationship. For example, if a client has had a poor attachment experience, then he is likely to develop the core belief, among others, that 'People are not trustworthy'. It is highly likely that he will carry that belief with him into therapy and that 'incidents' will happen in which lack of trust in the therapist will occur. These 'incidents' offer golden opportunities to work in the session on the client's immediate thoughts and schemata about trust. The interpersonal tangles resulting from such schemata can be relatively safely worked through in therapy, as illustrated by the further example of Jane's therapy.

> Jane was able to see the origin of her 'people-pleasing' and how it was driven by a lack of self-validation and self-esteem. She also detected the dysfunctional assumption that 'I must work harder and harder to please people if I am to ever get respect and recognition'. Her people-pleasing style was active in therapy in her 'pleasing' behaviour towards the therapist in the session. The therapist's supervisor advised him to look at how Jane could be a little more playful both with her colleagues and with the therapist. With statements like 'I bet I really get up your nose', Jane could express empathy for others and, at the same time, get some useful feedback from them. Jane's pattern was so ingrained that it took some time for her to be able to stay with the experiment of being 'playful', firstly with the therapist and then with her colleagues at work. Yet eventually she did begin to get experiential and emotional disconfirmation of her belief. One day she refused to clear up the office. She sought feedback from a colleague by asking, 'I bet that surprised you, didn't' it?' The colleague laughed and said that people would respect her more if she surprised them more often.

Conclusion

Barely 30 years old, cognitive therapy is still very much the 'new kid on the block' in the world of established psychotherapy and counselling models. Given its recent arrival, it has already shown a great vibrancy and capacity to develop very quickly. Cognitive therapy has also shown a capacity to listen to criticism, and change where appropriate. Although constructivist and schema-focused models of cognitive therapy seem to have many differences from the original model, such as described above, they also carry much of the older paradigm with them. For example, it is indeed debatable whether a true reading of Beck's earlier works does sustain the later accusations of being over-rational (Weishaar, 1993). It is probably more accurate to see the different ways of working as being on a continuum. Rather than replacing the old, newer approaches represent an extension of the original model which allows cognitive therapy to tackle a broader range of problems. The newer models have been put forward as being particularly appropriate for those difficulties with which the older model was not so successful – especially when clients have more disrupted and traumatic histories and more fundamental person-ality issues rather than supposedly straightforward emotional disorders. Whether it is possible to make such an easy distinction, or indeed to make any meaningful distinction, is an issue which we will consider when we return to a fuller description of the schema-focused model in Chapter 6.

2
Case Conceptualisation – At the Heart of Cognitive Therapy

There has been a tendency for therapeutic models to polarise between those which emphasise therapy as an experiential encounter, and those which stress therapy as a process wherein techniques are applied to a problem. As we have described in Chapter 1, initial models of cognitive therapy tended to locate themselves within the latter tradition. However, as the cognitive approach has evolved, the concept of case conceptualisation or formulation (the two words carry the same meaning and are used interchangeably) has enabled us to integrate different aspects of therapy: experiential and technical information about the client's difficulties and the process of therapy. Whilst case conceptualisation was implicit in the older models of cognitive therapy, the conceptualisation or formulation model has become much clearer in recent years. Beck et al. (1979, 1985) stress the importance of having an overall conceptualisation of the case; however, the approach of linking presenting problems to underlying psychological mechanisms was expanded by Jacqueline Persons (1989) and has subsequently developed, both in its application to specific problems, and in its integration of concepts concerning the role of emotion (Greenberg and Safran, 1984, 1987) and the therapeutic relationship (Layden et al., 1993; Safran and Segal, 1990). In cognitive therapy, the conceptualisation becomes the central driving force of the therapy process – a guide for understanding new material, the choice of strategies and the therapeutic relationship itself.

In this chapter, we look at what is meant by a case conceptualisation in cognitive therapy, and the value of conceptualisation. Cognitive case formulation goes on at many levels and this chapter will proceed by looking at the 'basic-level' conceptualisation, focusing on the client's immediate problems in terms of an interaction between thoughts, feelings, behaviour and biology as well as the individual's environment. We then go on to look at the conceptualisation of past experience, and the client's schemata and assumptions which may be 'running the show'. It will end by bringing these different levels into an overall conceptualisation. We look at some of the 'off the shelf' conceptualisations which are increasingly developing in cognitive therapy, and finally discuss some of the hazards of using case conceptualisation.

What is a Cognitive Case Conceptualisation?

There are many models of case conceptualisation in the cognitive therapy literature (for example, Beck et al., 1990; Blackburn and Davidson, 1995; Freeman, 1992; Freeman et al., 1990; Hawton et al., 1989; Kirk, 1989; Persons, 1989, 1993; Turkat and Maisto, 1985; Young, 1994). In its most basic form, a cognitive case conceptualisation is a means of understanding an individual's problems and distress in terms of the cognitive model of emotional disorders (Beck et al., 1979, 1985). The conceptualisation describes and operationalises the factors which maintain the individual's problems, and the underlying mechanisms which may predispose the client to developing the problems (Persons, 1989; Turkat and Maisto, 1985). As we have seen in Chapter 1, the cognitive model, in brief, proposes that thoughts and feelings are interrelated. At its simplest, a cognitive conceptualisation focuses on vicious cycles linking thoughts and emotions (p. 14). The conceptualisation also includes behaviour and biology, and how these impact on and are affected by thoughts and emotions. As well as looking at the problems the client is bringing to therapy, a conceptualisation also enables an understanding of problems in terms of underlying psychological mechanisms, namely assumptions and beliefs the client holds about him/herself, others and the world (Beck, 1976; Beck et al., 1979, 1985).

Case conceptualisation is an active and continuing process of developing a working hypothesis to provide a map or overview of the individual's problems and their origins. The map, made collaboratively with the client, is open to continuous modification, but acts as a useful guideline to any issue that crops up either in the client's life outside the therapy, or in the counselling relationship itself, and can act as the 'therapist's compass' (Persons, 1989). A good conceptualisation helps the client answer questions such as 'Why me?' 'Why now?' and 'Why doesn't the problem just go away?', as well as 'How can I get better?'

What is the Value of Case Conceptualisation in Cognitive Therapy?

> *If the formulation is so helpful to the therapist, we might also expect it to be helpful to the patient in understanding and managing his behaviour. Thus many of the interventions . . . are directed towards teaching the patient the nature of his central problem. (Persons, 1989, p. 48)*

Case conceptualisation is of importance for a number of reasons. It provides a bridge between the theory and practice of cognitive therapy, and helps make sense of the client's problems. Conceptualisation in itself is therapeutic, being a means of understanding, predicting and normalising the client's problems. Case conceptualisation provides a structure to therapy and guides the choice of interventions and treatments. It aids collaboration and is a means of dealing with problems in the process of therapy. Conceptualisation is also useful in dealing with the therapists' own problems and issues (Beck et al., 1979, 1985; Persons, 1989, 1993). In these and other ways, the case conceptualisation 'drives' the therapy.

1. Conceptualisation: Making Crystal out of Mud

Case conceptualisation is a means of linking the theory and practice of cognitive therapy. Theories of cognitive therapy are relatively clear and simple. In practice, we are dealing with the complexities of people. Our clients arrive with a mass of problems, seemingly intractable, incomprehensible, unending and unpredictable. If the client's problems are well conceptualised, she becomes more understandable and predictable both to herself and to the therapist. The client is likely to feel understood, and the therapist will feel more empathic towards her, thereby improving the therapeutic relationship (Mearns and Dryden, 1990). Case conceptualisation can be a powerful therapeutic method in itself. The process of clarification and differentiation between problems, defining apparently unrelated problems as part of one issue, or conceptualising a mass of issues into a smaller number of problems, helps the client make sense of the problems and believe that change is possible (Kirk, 1989). Conceptualisation is likely to increase the client's sense of understanding and control over her problems, and predicts future problems, thereby giving her the scope to avoid setbacks or relapse (Turkat and Maisto, 1985). An accurate conceptualisation of the client's difficulties aids understanding the picture for the individual client rather than making generalisations based on a more general diagnosis. For example, two clients may be terrified of fainting. One may fear fainting because it would indicate that there was something seriously wrong, indicating beliefs about the meaning of physical symptoms or themes of vulnerability. The other client feared fainting because she would make a fool of herself and lose others' respect. Thus, one very common symptom or problem has very different meanings depending on the individual, which need to be understood in terms of differing psychological mechanisms.

2. Conceptualisation Focuses and Guides Counselling

For any problem, a range of therapeutic strategies are available. For example, it is not unusual for clients to bring to therapy a range of seemingly unrelated problems. Whilst one strategy might be to throw solutions at the various problems in the hope that one or more might prove effective, the client may become discouraged and some interventions may be counterproductive. A more effective method is to base the choice of approach on an understanding of both the overt problems and the underlying mechanisms. The conceptualisation is therefore a means of structuring and focusing therapy and enabling decisions to be made about the choice of intervention strategies and even which questions to ask during the process of guided discovery detailed in Chapter 5 (Blackburn and Davidson, 1995; Freeman, 1992; Persons, 1989; Turkat and Carlson, 1984). For example, relaxation is a frequently advocated treatment for anxiety. For an individual whose anxiety can be conceptualised by a belief that relaxing and letting go is dangerous, learning progressive muscular relaxation to activate and challenge the belief may be useful. However, for another client who believes 'If I'm anxious, I may die', relaxation may be counterproductive, in that always relaxing when feeling anxious prevents the client finding out that anxiety, whilst unpleasant, is not terminal (Salkovskis, 1991). The conceptualisation can therefore guide the choice of the many approaches to treating anxiety and worry (Beck et al., 1985).

3. Conceptualisation Aids Collaboration and Helps Deal with Problems in Therapy

Working with a case conceptualisation actively involves the client in therapy and improves collaboration. By learning how to conceptualise problems, the client becomes his own therapist. An understanding of underlying mechanisms alerts him to unhelpful attitudes and beliefs, as well as teaching strategies for solving problems.

The conceptualisation enables the therapist to understand and predict difficulties in therapy and 'off the ball' incidents which occur in therapy, such as persistent lateness or non-attendance, or the client not doing homework. Such issues or difficulties can be conceptualised in terms of the clients' overall picture, as understandable problems for both client and therapist, collaboratively, to work on. The conceptualisation helps clients and therapists to consider how particular moves and interventions will influence the overall pattern of therapy. The case conceptualisation approach helps the therapist understand and work with difficulties in the therapeutic relationship, by assuming that the client's behaviour with the therapist is similar to behaviour with others, and that both are driven by the central underlying problem (Persons, 1989). It also allows consideration of how the therapeutic relationship will unfold. For example, if interpersonal schemata regarding dependence are active in the client's life, this can be allowed for or even used in therapy, by discussing how her dependence might be successfully overcome by working through a well-planned and resolving end to therapy.

4. Conceptualisation for Therapists
As well as conceptualising our clients, case conceptualisation can also be usefully applied to therapists. By conceptualising ourselves and our reactions to our clients, we can work with difficulties we have with particular clients or particular clinical problems (Persons, 1989). If the therapist shares the same, not altogether functional, beliefs as the client, then it can be difficult for either to see or predict difficulties or blocks in therapy, and the therapist may unwittingly 'collude' with, rather than challenge, the client's assumptions. Again to use the example of anxiety: if the therapist personally finds anxiety a difficult, threatening emotion, believing 'I must be in control at all times' or 'Anxiety is dangerous', she is likely to be tempted to guide the client towards managing anxious feelings rather than exploring their meaning. Having a conceptualisation of our own views of clients' issues may be a way of avoiding such collusion.

The method of case conceptualisation is also very valuable to therapists in that it enables the therapist to work with a variety of problems which s/he may not have encountered before. Although the problems may seem different, applying a general method of case conceptualisation is applicable over a wide range of work in therapy.

Case Conceptualisation in Practice

Developing a cognitive case conceptualisation is an ongoing process throughout the course of therapy. It often starts even before client and therapist meet. The therapist may have information about the client from referral letters, discussion with colleagues, a body of knowledge about the problem based on training and experience, and information from contact with the client, such as telephone calls or difficulties in making an appointment. Likewise, the client will have an understanding of his problem based on his experience and knowledge, reading, previous experience of psychological therapies and discussions with others. Both therapists' and clients' assumptions about the problems can be a rich source of material for the conceptualisation, or may equally be a rich source of misinformation that needs revising.

Conceptualisation: A Shared Process

At all stages, a conceptualisation is a working hypothesis, which may or may not be useful to both client and counsellor. We have seen how conceptualisation aims to help the counsellor think about how things fit together, what might change and what the difficulties of change might be. Conceptualisation also needs to have exactly the same functions for the client. Hence, cognitive therapy leans towards trying to share as much of the conceptualisation with the client as possible. In many instances, the client can be given a full diagram (as shown later in the chapter) at an early stage of therapy to play with and reformulate as therapy proceeds and her own ideas develop. The conceptualisation can also be simplified or otherwise tailored to individual client need, with elements of the model used as we have done throughout this chapter. There are sometimes reasons not to look at the full conceptualisation until later in therapy – perhaps some clients might not be able to follow it or, at the other extreme, some clients might treat it as an excuse to 'intellectualise' about their issues. Also, the therapist may hold some hypotheses about the client's underlying schema or experience, which it may be counterproductive to focus on too early in therapy, possibly because the issues raised would be too painful for the client to deal with all at once. We, however, believe that most clients are able to make good use of a conceptualisation and would encourage counsellors to err on the side of sharing. Overall, sharing and discussing the conceptualisation with the client is an integral and important part of the therapy process. It is also a means of working collaboratively with the client, and introducing him, at an early stage, into the process of collaborative empiricism.

Conceptualisation: A Written Exercise

Cognitive therapists are never without pen and paper, and, ideally, a white board. Cognitive therapy has most things 'out on the table' or illustrated in a written form. The conceptualisation, as well as key points of the therapy, are illustrated, in black and white, during the session, for both client and counsellor to think about during and between sessions. There are many ways of illustrating a conceptualisation, such as vicious cycles, pictures or metaphors (Freeman, 1992) or ready-made conceptualisations with computer-generated boxes to fill in negative automatic thoughts and underlying beliefs. Literally drawing out a diagram of the conceptualisation is a very useful activity for clients. It can begin to trace out patterns and chains of different reactions in a readily understandable way and offer a way of finding a point where intervention and change can begin.

Basic Conceptualisation: Linking Thoughts, Feelings, Behaviour and Biology

One very important point about case conceptualisation is that, at the beginning of therapy, the most useful conceptualisations can be made by asking the client for a specific, concrete, recent and severe example of the problem brought to therapy: rather than asking 'How do you generally feel . . .?', asking 'Can you describe in detail a recent example of . . .?' This way, the conceptualisation can be specific, concrete and relevant to the client's concerns.

The Thought–Emotion Cycle

One of the aims in basic conceptualisation is to begin to look at the *meaning* the client is giving to situations, emotions or biology, expressed as the client's 'negative automatic thoughts'. The essence of the model is that emotional difficulties begin when the way we see events gets exaggerated beyond the available evidence; these exaggerated ways of seeing things tend to have negative influences on our feelings and behaviour, in a *vicious cycle*. For example, appraising meeting people as 'worrying' raises anxiety and primes us for evasive, defensive or other reaction. Rather than the anxiety being functional, if we start to become preoccupied with the risks of meeting people, and begin to see ourselves making *faux pas*, then our emotion of slight, functional anxiety becomes one of unease or even panic. Furthermore, if this feeling increases, the chances of our making *faux pas* may increase, which further increases our anxiety and so maintains the problem.

Therefore, following the model, in the first stages of conceptualisation, the counsellor and client work together to come up with the links between thoughts, affect, behaviour and biology specific to the individual. The aim is to begin to draw out the client's specific thoughts and emotions, looking in particular at how each relates to the other. This forms the rudimentary conceptualisation in cognitive therapy, as the following brief dialogue with a depressed client illustrates:

> *Counsellor*: So, yesterday, you were finding it difficult to write your essay. What was going through your mind?
> *Client*: I kept thinking 'I'm such a failure: a useless failure.'
> *Counsellor*: And when you say to yourself 'I'm a useless failure', how does that make you feel?
> *Client*: Terrible, really depressed.
> *Counsellor*: And when you feel really depressed, what goes through your mind?
> *Client*: . . . I'm such a useless failure.

This kind of dialogue leads to the simplest level conceptualisation, linking the client's specific thoughts with feelings, leading to a drawing such as shown in Figure 2.1.

Expanding the Cycle: The Role of Behaviour
The next section of the vicious cycle, often identified and drawn up at the same time as the simple level conceptualisation described above, is to begin to add behaviour and biology to the equation. For example, a common pattern with depression is that people will become withdrawn, not going out or staying in bed for long periods. At these times, they often feel a lot worse – the ease of rest does not work. The inactivity gives more opportunity to think, which seems to easily turn to moping and morbid rumination – including negative thoughts about the self for

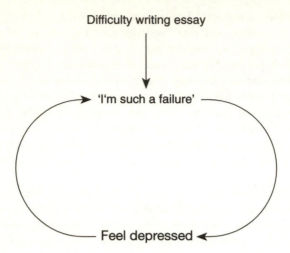

Figure 2.1   *Linking thoughts and feelings*

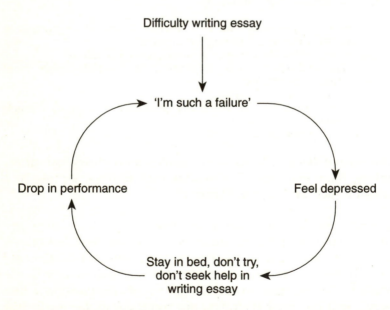

Figure 2.2   *Linking thoughts, feelings and behaviour*

staying in bed. For our client above, the cycle can be expanded as illustrated in Figure 2.2.

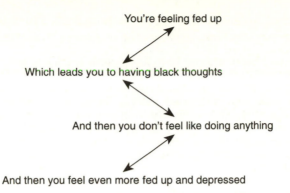

You're feeling fed up

Which leads you to having black thoughts

And then you don't feel like doing anything

And then you feel even more fed up and depressed

Figure 2.3 *Linking thoughts, feelings and behaviour*

A further example is given below.

John is a 52-year-old farm labourer. He has had considerable family problems with two of his four sons getting in trouble with the law. His marriage has been very strained, with his wife spending long periods with her sister in a nearby village. John became withdrawn and very depressed – unlike his old, generally quite cheerful, self. His GP asked the practice counsellor to try to help but warned that he might not be very psychologically minded. The counsellor found him easy to get on with and they began to make some progress on helping him understand his depression by drawing and discussing the diagram shown in Figure 2.3.

Avoidance is a very common, and important, behaviour which maintains a number of problems, particularly anxiety. The individual avoids going into situations just in case something bad happens, such as not going out of the house in case of collapsing, or avoiding social situations which provoke anxiety. Not doing what is feared will, in the short term, alleviate anxiety; however, in the long term, avoidance prevents the individual from learning how to deal with situations, or even learn that what is feared is very unlikely to happen, and erodes the individual's confidence.

Adding Biology to Complete the Cycle
The fourth stage in developing a conceptualisation is to bring in the client's physical symptoms or somatic state. In anxiety, physical symptoms often predominate: the initial problem may be conceptualised by anxious clients as 'There's something wrong with my body: I'm ill'. The aim of conceptualisation is to help the client to look at how the physical feelings interact and trigger off

the other components of the cycle, well illustrated by the cognitive model of panic (Clark, 1989), as the following demonstrates.

Mavis had been referred from her general practitioner for help with anxiety and panic attacks. Mavis had not initially thought about the possibility that she was anxious, and did not know what a panic attack was. She had been feeling awful, with 'out of the blue' episodes of shaking, difficulty in breathing, tight chestedness and tingling in her arms. She was extremely concerned that this was the beginnings of heart disease, and had been checked up by the cardiologist, who had diagnosed anxiety and sent Mavis off to 'sort herself out'.

The counsellor asked Mavis to describe a recent example of feeling awful, in this case in the supermarket. The conceptualisation proceeded as follows:

Counsellor: What was the first thing you noticed?
Mavis: I started to feel awful: really odd, completely out of the blue. I couldn't breathe, I started to get these pains in my chest and the tingling . . . I felt quite shaky.
Counsellor: So, you were feeling really awful . . . when you felt like this, what was going through your mind?
Mavis: Well, I know it's stupid since I know there's nothing wrong with me: the cardiologist said so . . . but I really thought I was having a heart attack and this was it!
Counsellor: It sounds like you were feeling pretty bad, but you sound a bit embarrassed about what you made of it . . . I guess it makes sense if you were feeling that bad.
Mavis: um . . .
Counsellor: So, you felt awful, chest pains, couldn't breathe, and you said to yourself, 'I'm having a heart attack . . . this is it'. When you said that to yourself, how did that make you feel?
Mavis: Terrified.
Counsellor: And when you felt terrified, what was going on in your body?
Mavis: I guess it didn't help: I felt much worse.

The counsellor writes down the sequence as illustrated in Figure 2.4.

The formulation of panic also stresses the role of behaviour: what the client does in order to prevent the feared catastrophe, such as stopping, sitting down, breathing heavily to avoid a heart attack. These have been called 'safety behaviours' which, whilst well meant, may actually exacerbate the client's problems and so become a focus for therapy (Salkovskis, 1991). In Mavis's example, the counsellor asked her what she did to prevent herself having a heart attack, identified as sitting down, escaping from the

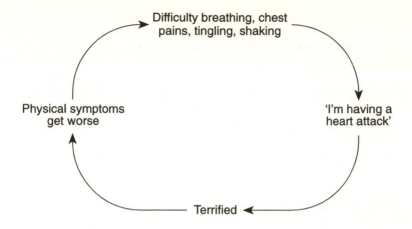

Figure 2.4 *Linking thoughts, feelings, behaviour and biology*

situation and breathing deeply, behaviours which can then be added to the conceptualisation.

Conceptualising Environmental, Social and Cultural Factors

All therapies aim to emphasise the unique qualities of the individual, and to understand the issues the client brings into therapy in terms of an overall, or holistic, picture. As we have seen, cognitive case conceptualisation seeks to understand the hows and whys of the difficulties the client has been experiencing, in terms of overall functioning in the present and in terms of past experience. Psychotherapies as a whole have been criticised for not paying sufficient attention to the wider social and cultural context in which the individual operates, and cognitive therapy is no exception (Hays, 1995). Therefore the conceptualisation must always take into account the client's cultural background: 'The culturally responsive practice of cognitive-behavior therapy demands that the client's values be recognised and respected, which in turn means that the problem must be defined in relation to the client's cultural norms' (Hays, 1995, p. 313). Hays goes on to remind us: 'although cognitive-behavior therapy theoretically acknowledges the variability in definitions of adaptive and mal-adaptive behaviour, in reality, Euro-American norms and values have dominated its practice' (1995, p. 313). The issues of culture and psychotherapy are too large to pay anything but lip service to here. However, any conceptualisation must both take into account and sit comfortably with the client's culture. In practice, for example, women clients often express beliefs about themselves, others and the world which are common to many women and are culturally proscribed and reinforced. A good conceptualisation seeks to understand the individual's psychology in terms of not only their unique experience but the experience of being a woman in the 1990s.

Environmental factors, too, are of vital importance in determining how we react in the world and the meaning given to situations. Socially isolated women with young children are at particular risk of depression; mental health correlates strongly with economic factors. The conceptualisation must consider these, and remind ourselves and our clients that we do not operate in isolation, and therefore any change has to take into account the wider social and cultural context.

Other Models of Conceptualisation

Cognitive conceptualisation may be as varied as our clients, and require creativity on the part of the therapist. Not all problems fit into vicious cycles, or straight lines; for some clients, behaviour, biology or even thoughts may play little role in the conceptualisation. For example, clients with somatic problems (Sanders, 1996) and chronic fatigue syndrome (Surawy et al., 1995) appear not to have any negative thoughts or emotions; therefore trying to sell a model linking thoughts and affect is likely to be unhelpful. The therapist's challenge is to be sufficiently flexible and creative to develop a workable conceptualisation with the client that takes into account what she is saying and believing, regardless of whether it fits into the cognitive model in the therapist's head.

A generic model, shown in Figure 2.5, is a means of integrating thoughts, emotions, behaviour and biology as well as the effect of the environment (Padesky and Mooney, 1990). The model illustrates the impact of the different components on each other and means that wherever the client starts to describe his problems, the therapist can look at the other components and include these in the conceptualisation. For example, a client who says that his problem of depression is 'all biological' can be asked about how biology affects mood, which in turn affects thoughts, which in

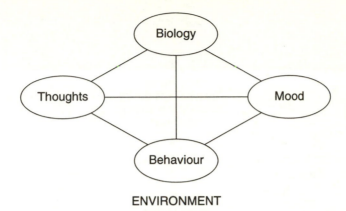

ENVIRONMENT

© 1986 Center for Cognitive Therapy, Newport Beach, CA.

Figure 2.5   *Generic model (reproduced with permission from Padesky and Mooney, 1990)*

turn affects behaviour. The model allows all aspects of the client's functioning to be included in the conceptualisation.

The generic model was valuable in engaging Philip in cognitive therapy. Philip, a 50-year-old man who had been depressed for two years, had only reluctantly agreed to see the psychologist in his doctor's surgery to talk about his problems. Antidepressant medication had not proved all that helpful, and Philip was still very low. Initially, he was adamant that his problems were due to chemical imbalances in his brain, and therefore psychological factors were not relevant. The therapist developed a model of Philip's problems as follows:

Philip: I really don't see much point in talking about it. Depression is an illness – it's the chemicals in my brain that need fixing. I don't know what else to do about it.

Therapist: Yes, there's no doubt that depression is a chemical imbalance. But, it may be that there are other things you can do to help, despite what's causing the depression. Would you be happy to talk a bit more about it to see if there are any other ways of tackling the depression.

Philip: Well, OK . . .

Therapist: Tell me a bit about how you've been feeling.

Philip: Really low: I've no energy and I just can't get on and do anything. I just want to sleep all the time.

Therapist: So, the depression is making you feel very tired so it's hard to get on with anything. How does the tiredness make you feel in yourself?

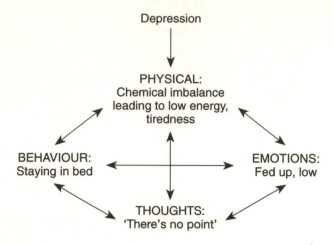

Figure 2.6   *Generic model for Philip*

Philip: Very fed up really. Like there's not much point in anything.
Therapist: It sounds like you've been feeling very fed up, and that makes you say 'There's no point'. When you say that to yourself, how does that make you feel?
Philip: More fed up, I guess.
Therapist: And when you feel fed up, what do you want to do?
Philip: I just want to sleep.
Therapist: [*Summarising*] I've been drawing up a model as you've been talking. What you've told me is that the depression is making you feel very low: the chemicals really affect your energy levels. When you feel physically low, you want to sleep all the time, which makes you feel low and tired, and feeling low makes you think there's no point, which makes you feel fed up [*draws up diagram – Figure 2.6*].
Philip: I see: all the bits connect together.
Therapist: Yes: what this model might show is that whatever causes the depression, it affects not only how you feel, but also what you say to yourself, your thoughts, and what you do: which in turn has an effect on you physically.

As a result of using the diagram, Philip agreed to try to tackle the depression in different aspects, such as working out ways of behaving differently when depressed, and looking at his patterns of thinking.

Another clinically valuable conceptualisation is the 'vicious daisy', where the central problem is maintained by a number of 'petals' made up of different maintaining factors. For example, a client's thoughts, feelings and behaviour may be both the result and cause of low self-esteem, as illustrated in Figure 2.7. The

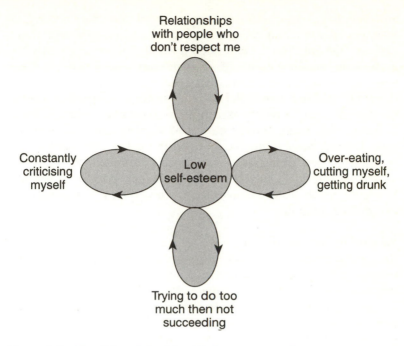

Figure 2.7   *The vicious daisy (Ann Hackmann, personal communication, 1996)*

model shows that, as a result of low self-esteem, the client picks unhealthy relationships, abuses herself in various ways, attempts impossible tasks and castigates herself for not succeeding, and continually gives herself very negative messages: all of which reinforce her lack of self-esteem. Petal diagrams are used by Salkovskis to conceptualise obsessional problems and health anxiety (Salkovskis and Bass, 1996).

Conceptualising Dysfunctional Assumptions and Core Beliefs: A Longitudinal Perspective

So far we have discussed conceptualising the links between the client's thinking and emotions, and the role of behaviour and biology to complete the picture. The next stage in developing a case conceptualisation is to begin to conceptualise the problems in terms of underlying psychological mechanisms, namely dysfunctional assumptions and beliefs which are related to, and which 'drive', the negative automatic thoughts and affect. Assumptions and beliefs can be understood in terms of the client's early, or later, experiences, and cultural, biological and environmental factors, as relevant. The client's fleeting thoughts are often only the immediate manifestations of deeper cognitive levels. If these thoughts are seen as the branches of the tree, then assumptions are the trunk and the core beliefs related to early experience are the roots of the tree. In reality assumptions and beliefs often go hand in hand, each using similar means of identification and challenging. Indeed, there is some debate on the value of separating the two, and Jeffrey Young's schema-focused approach (Young, 1994) views assumptions and beliefs as a wider part of schemata. However, for the sake of illustration, we will look at assumptions and beliefs separately.

What are Beliefs and Assumptions?

We all have beliefs and assumptions about ourselves, others and the world. Such beliefs and assumptions may be thought of as our frame of reference, or set of rules determining our 'way of being' in the world, how we judge ourselves, situations or others, and how we interact with other people (Beck, 1976). Our rules are formed mainly from our early experience, and often become revised as we develop and encounter different experiences. Rules generally operate without us being aware of them. We selectively pay attention to the world around us, screening, sorting and integrating information according to our rules. Core beliefs, or schemata, are often expressed in absolute terms such as 'I am a bad person', 'I'm a failure', 'I'm vulnerable' or 'I'm worthless'. As well as beliefs about the self, schemata cover beliefs about others, such as 'Other people can never be trusted', and beliefs about the world such as 'The world is a dangerous place'. Assumptions, in contrast, are often conditional, 'if . . . then' statements, developed to some extent in order to enable the individual to live with the particular beliefs. For example, the individual who felt herself to be a bad person, may develop a rule: 'If I am nice all the time, and put others' needs first, then they won't see what a bad person I am', or for an individual who believes 'I am a failure', an assumption may develop such as 'I must be perfect and in control of everything . . . to make a mistake means I'm a complete failure'. Beck (1996) identifies three types of conditional rules: negative conditional rules ('if I get close to others, they will reject me'); compensating conditional rules ('if I avoid others, I can avoid rejection'); and imperative rules ('I must be perfect').

Assumptions and beliefs which may underlie emotional problems have been labelled 'dysfunctional' or 'maladaptive'. In practice, our set of rules may well have been functional and adaptive at some stage in life. For example, it may have been useful for the child to believe 'I am responsible for bad things happening' and 'If I am extremely careful and do everything just right, then bad things may not happen', in order to survive childhood abuse, rather than risking rejection from parents. Problems may arise, however, when our rules are not adjusted and revised in the light of later experience, or when we take on board rules that are the result of someone else's distorted or unhelpful way of seeing things: in the above example, the individual's rules may lead to obsessional problems and a great deal of self-blame or disgust. Therefore, terms such as 'unhelpful' or 'out-of-date' assumptions or beliefs may be more realistic and less judgemental.

Unhelpful assumptions and beliefs have various characteristics (Fennell, 1989). Assumptions are a set of rules that are learned through experience. They often 'run in families' in one form or another. Many are culturally reinforced, meeting gender or cultural stereotypes which make it difficult for the individual to identify or challenge the beliefs. Unhelpful assumptions often fit into three themes: achievement, acceptance and control (Beck et al., 1985). Examples may include 'In order to be happy, I must be successful in everything'; 'To be happy I must be accepted by all people at all time';'If someone disagrees with me, it must mean I'm an awful person';'If I am nice and never angry, bad things won't happen';'I must be in control all the time'. Assumptions are often unconscious. We are not aware of the rules themselves, only the emotional or physical discomfort that may arise from transgressing them. For example, an individual whose rule says 'I need to be perfect in everything I do in order to be acceptable' will feel excessive anxiety or depression on making a seemingly small mistake.

Deeply held beliefs and assumptions exert an ongoing influence on how we perceive and behave in our worlds. An individual who believes, for example, 'I am a failure' may have many examples throughout life to prove that this belief is distorted; however, we have subtle ways of discounting and ignoring information which does not confirm our beliefs whilst collecting and remembering instances where the belief is confirmed. We look more at the process of how beliefs are maintained throughout life in Chapter 6. Young (1994) describes the process of 'schema maintenance', whereby our beliefs become self-fulfilling prophecies, and we pay attention to information or behave in a manner which confirms our beliefs and discount, ignore or alter information which disconfirms the belief. The process has been compared to that of a prejudice (Padesky, 1993b): however much the world, our experience or other people disconfirm our rules, we may carry on believing our beliefs, reinforced through select-ive attention, distorting of information to fit the facts, and ignor-ing contrary information. For example, a room may be filled with 99 people offering praise and encouragement, whereas one is muttering how badly the job was done. The perfectionist or the individual whose self-worth is determined by others' views notices only the mutterings of one, filtering out or not even noticing the vast majority.

Conceptualising Assumptions
In reality, the stage of identifying and conceptualising assump-tions often runs in parallel with the development of a basic-level conceptualisation. It is, however, developed more fully during the later stages of therapy. It involves looking at more general prin-ciples and themes involved in the client's problems as well as working with specific examples characteristic of the earlier stages of therapy. Thematic guides are useful to the therapist in tracking down assumptions. The information for identifying underlying psychological mechanisms comes from many different sources including the presenting problems, themes in therapy, diaries of negative automatic thoughts, questionnaires, the client's response to therapy or the therapist, and issues in the therapy process (Beck et al., 1990; Freeman, 1992; Persons, 1989; Turkat and Maisto, 1985; Young, 1994). We describe these approaches in greater detail in Chapter 5. An excellent technique to use in this endeavour is the 'downward arrow', described by Burns (1980) and Fennell (1989). Here the therapist picks up the negative automatic thought and keeps asking questions like, 'And if that were true, what would that mean?' in order to reach the silent assumption/s underlying it. The following illustrates this technique:

> *Client*: If I keep falling behind, I'll be right out of favour . . .
> *Therapist*: And if you were right out of favour, what would that mean to you?
> *Client*: I'd be likely to lose my job altogether.
> *Therapist*: And if you did lose your job altogether, what would be the worst thing about it?
> *Client*: I'd have failed my wife and kids.

Therapist: And If you do fail your wife and kids . . . what would that mean to you?

Client: They'd leave me . . . I'd be a complete failure . . . a wreck.

The final assumption reached is usually of an 'if . . . then' format. It can be either positive or negative form – taking the above example, the positive form is: 'If I can hold onto people, then I'm not a failure', the negative form being 'If people leave me then I am a failure'.

Assumptions lie around waiting to be triggered. If the person's life is going well, particular assumptions may hardly ever be triggered. If there is potential significant failure or the impending loss of an important person, then a salient assumption may well be triggered. At this moment, the person is not only dealing with the emotion that anyone would feel when they appear to fail, but is also dealing with the latent negative feeling contained within the assumption. This double effect explains the strength of the resulting feelings. A conceptualisation in terms of underlying assumptions can help the client to understand more about these strong feelings and thus be less frightened of them. As previously, drawing out these patterns with pen and paper can help the client face and work with these strong feelings and therefore can move the therapy forward. For example, a client Sydney had the assumption: 'If I can please people, I might win their respect'. When his colleagues at work showed even minor irritation with him, he had the automatic thoughts: 'They think I'm crap . . . they hate me'. This triggered his assumption, along with the thought: 'I'll never win their respect'. He then felt overwhelmed with negative feeling to the extent that his work deteriorated, eliciting yet further negative signals from his colleagues. The chain of events was discussed and drawn out on paper, as shown in Figure 2.8.

In Sydney's example, the assumption leads to a stream of thoughts whenever activated; it is also clear that the assumption may act as a 'self-fulfilling prophecy' in that trying to please people all the time and trying too hard may well provoke irritation from others, as well as lead to a deterioration of performance.

Conceptualising Core Beliefs

Core beliefs and schemata are the deepest level of cognition, underlying both automatic thoughts and assumptions. Whereas assumptions are 'if . . . then' conditional rules, core beliefs are

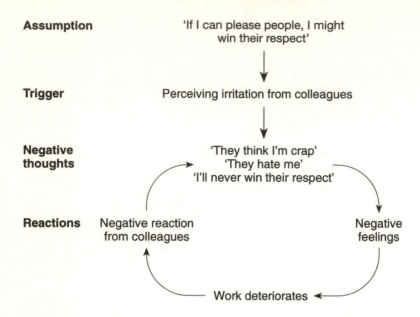

Figure 2.8 *Conceptualising assumptions*

absolute – 'I am bad', 'I'll never find anyone who could love me', 'Nobody can be trusted'. They are so negative and tyrannical that they are very hard to live with. Hence assumptions develop which, whilst in themselves may not be totally helpful or functional, at least mitigate the effects of the core belief. Core beliefs are not only about the self, but are about wider concerns: about other people and the world. For example, 'People are never to be trusted' and 'The world is a dangerous unsafe place' lead the individual to be over-vigilant and have a heightened sense of vulnerability. Beliefs are often more rigid and resistant to change than are assumptions, and appear from the outside as extreme, irrational and unreasonable. They are relatively impervious to ordinary experience, and are treated as a fact not as a belief. They may be expressed in very clear, simple, black and white language: 'I'm bad', 'I'm weak', It's wrong to lose control'. The words may be those of a child, representing primitive and undeveloped meanings which clearly do not reflect the attributes or skills of the individual. They are often unhelpful and not functional, preventing the individual achieving his goals in life.

The conceptualisation of core beliefs provides a bridge between cognitive therapy and other forms of therapy which give prominence to the client's early experience. Whilst early forms of cognitive therapy may have reacted against psychoanalytic therapy by developing a suspicion of exploring the past experience of clients, Beck, right from the start of his work, has always reserved an important role for past experience, specifically in the way that the client has drawn certain conclusions about life, other people and herself based on her experiences of the same (Beck et al., 1979). Therefore, as part of conceptualising the client's past experience, when reviewing the client's history, an important question for client and therapist to explore is: 'What conclusions do you think you drew about yourself, others and the world, based on what happened to you at that time?'

The Full Conceptual Model

Whilst the above description of the process may sound like putting together pieces of a jigsaw bit by bit, in practice the process is more organic and flexible, conceptualisation being a *process* that runs through the whole of therapy. We usually start with the basic-level conceptualisation, putting together the pieces with the client; however, in our minds is the wider model, thinking about what kind of underlying mechanisms are driving the problem, and the kinds of experience that might have led the client to develop such beliefs about the self, others and the world. The general model of case conceptualisation, modified from Fennell (1989) and Judith Beck (1995), is illustrated in Figure 2.9.

Another user-friendly version of the conceptual model is based on an expansion of the 'vicious daisy' model shown above (Figure 2.7). The petals represent what keeps the central problem in place: in the case of the illustration in Figure 2.10, the kinds of behaviour and emotion which contribute to the negative thinking. The stem of the daisy is the individual's beliefs and assumptions, which are 'rooted' in past experience (Ann Hackmann, personal communication, 1996). The daisy can also be conceptualised as being continually fed and watered by factors which maintain the person's difficulties, such as his pattern of thinking, behaviour and personal circumstances.

These detailed conceptualisations may be developed early on in therapy, or, in the case of clients with more complex, long-standing problems, may evolve over many sessions. As we have

---

Early Experience
Information about the client's early and other significant experiences
which may have shaped core beliefs and assumptions.

Development of Beliefs about the Self, Others and the World
Unconditional, core beliefs developing from early experience, such as
'I am bad', 'I am weak and vulnerable', 'Others will always look after
me' or 'The world is a dangerous place'.

Assumptions or Rules for Living
Conditional statements, often phrased as 'if . . . then' rules, to enable
the individual to function despite core beliefs: e.g. 'If I am vigilant
about my health at all times, then I'll be safe, despite being
vulnerable'; 'If I work hard all the time, I'll be OK, despite being a bad
person'.

Critical Incidents which Trigger Problems
Situations or events in which the rules are broken or assumptions are
activated.

Problem and Factors Maintaining the Problem
Physical symptoms, thoughts, emotions, behaviours interacting in a
'vicious cycle'.

Figure 2.9   *Cognitive conceptualisation (J. Beck, 1995; Fennell,
1989)*

described above, the process of developing a detailed conceptualisation may in itself be therapeutic, providing a blame-free understanding of why the client is as she is today, and also provides a
workable bridge between the present and the past.

Pret à Porter Formulations

Cognitive therapy provides an ever-increasing number of what
we might call 'ready-made' conceptualisations, where the problems clients are facing have been seen to fall into familiar patterns,
leading to the development of conceptualisations which may well
fit a range of people. For example, the model of panic shown in
Figure 2.4 is well known, well researched and familiar (Clark,

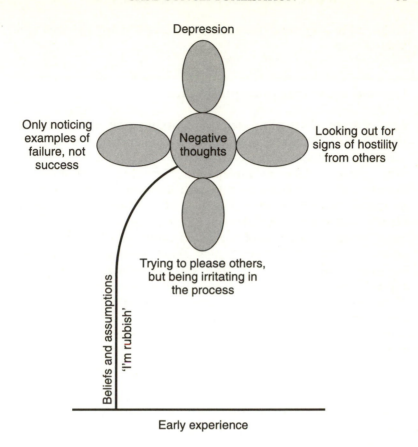

Figure 2.10   *The mature vicious daisy (Ann Hackman, personal communication, 1996)*

1989) and it is certainly our clinical experience that it is both descriptive of and valuable to a large number of our panicking clients. These conceptualisations guide what sense the therapist is making of the client's problems as well as the specific questions the therapist asks; similarly, being found to fit in with a familiar and well-established pattern can be helpful to the client, in so much as they feel relieved that 'I'm not the only one; if it makes sense, I'm not mad after all'.

A number of conceptual models are referenced throughout the book. New models are continually developed; old models are revised in the light of clinical and research experience, and readers are urged to keep up to date with cognitive therapy research and publications.

Cautions about Case Conceptualisation

Case conceptualisation is, ideally, a working map, which aims to improve both therapists' and clients' understanding of the client's problems, to guide the process of therapy, and to predict and deal with problems. Like any therapeutic process, it can be misused. Both therapist and client need to be flexible enough to throw out an initial conceptualisation if it does not fit with later evidence (Turkat and Maisto, 1985). However, it may be just as difficult for us as therapists to get rid of our beliefs about our clients as it is for clients to relinquish their beliefs about themselves. We may develop a perfect, sophisticated and theoretically sound conceptualisation which has little empirical or practical value to the client, and, because of our own cognitive distortions, start to see everything in those terms. There is a danger in attempting to be over-inclusive: whilst one conceptualisation may explain a number of problems, it is also possible that a number of different conceptualisations are necessary to work with disparate problems.

The conceptualisation is, by definition, influenced by the therapist's theoretical conceptualisations. An example of a conceptualisation based on minimal knowledge of the client and heavily determined by the therapist's model was provided in a recent allocation meeting at the health centre where I (DS) work. A young man's referral letter mentioned, amongst other things, that he was concerned about 'spots on his penis'. In my mind, I was busy formulating a cognitive model of hypochondriasis: the spots had always been there, but he had started to notice them during a time of heightened anxiety, fuelled by media reports of AIDS; he had then continued to pay attention to that area of his body, interpreted the spots as signs of serious illness, regularly checking to see if the spots were still there, so raising his anxiety, thus exacerbating and maintaining the problem. The psychodynamic therapist in the team formulated the problem by referring to 'the man with the sexual problems'. We were, no doubt, both premature in our formulations: the spots had, in fact, merely provided the client with an excuse to visit his doctor and talk about other, emotional problems.

Conclusion

Cognitive conceptualisation involves a delicate balance between holding in mind a conceptual model in which to slot the data generated by the client, and being open-minded to the information that the client is actually giving us. A further danger of the formulation is that therapists do have influence over clients, and we need to go out of our way to invite them to criticise or rebuke the formulation. This is particularly true when working at the level of schemata, where the views that the client holds about themselves, other people and the world are so firmly ingrained as to seem to be facts. Therefore formulating a client's underlying beliefs may lead him to retort 'Well, that's just the truth – it's how it is', being so confrontational to him as to lead to a great deal of either emotion or avoidance.

Similarly, whilst a conceptualisation provides a useful map, some of the most valuable journeys involve wandering off the chosen path.

3

The Therapeutic Relationship in Cognitive Therapy

One of the common criticisms of cognitive therapy from the counselling world is that cognitive therapists pay little, if any, attention to what is often the cornerstone of other therapies, the therapeutic relationship. Rogerians may accuse cognitive therapists of lacking empathy, merely applying a range of techniques in a somewhat mechanical manner and challenging the 'patient's dysfunctional thoughts' without regard for the individual's sensitivities. Psychoanalysts may dismiss cognitive therapy as not using the most important therapeutic tools of their trade, the transference and countertransference in the therapeutic relationship. Somehow, many writings on cognitive therapy give the impression that the therapeutic relationship is a mere container in which to do the real work, viewing difficulties and issues in the therapeutic relationship as problems to be solved before getting on with the therapy. The therapeutic relationship has been notable by its absence, at times seemingly dismissed.

We are glad to say that these views are, if not incorrect, at least anachronistic. The development of therapy in general has provided many useful ideas which help us to understand the underlying processes of therapeutic change within the therapeutic relationship, processes which are now being actively integrated into cognitive therapy. These include humanistic concepts of warmth and acceptance and psychodynamic concepts of transference and countertransference. These concepts can be relatively easily translated into cognitive work and this has been done by such writers as Safran and Segal (1990), Young (1994), Beck et al. (1990) and Layden et al. (1993). As a result, there is a growing cognitive model of the interpersonal process of the therapeutic relationship as well as substantial focus on how to use the relationship as an active ingredient in therapy. These issues have been particularly developed in the therapy of 'personality disorders' and 'schema-driven problems', where the client's transference, the therapist's countertransference and the experience of impasse in the therapeutic process all provide invaluable information for the facilitation of therapeutic movement.

In this chapter, we look at how the therapeutic relationship has been viewed in the past, and how recent work on cognitive therapy has brought the therapeutic relationship to centre stage, particularly for those clients with long-term difficulties, and those where relationships are of central concern. We look at ways the therapeutic relationship is used in cognitive therapy, 'in the service of therapy' (Safran and Segal, 1990, p. 41), to conceptualise the client's difficulties and facilitate the counselling process. Working with difficulties in the therapeutic relationship is covered in greater detail in Chapter 7.

What Does Cognitive Therapy Say about the Therapeutic Relationship?

> *The therapeutic relationship: 'Two people, both with problems in living, who agree to work together to study those problems, with the hope that the therapist has fewer problems than the patient.' (Harry Stack Sullivan, cited in Safran and Segal, 1990, p. 5)*

Traditionally, and in contrast to other therapeutic approaches, the task of cognitive therapy was seen to be to resolve the client's problems, as far as possible, using the tools of cognitive therapy rather than using the therapeutic relationship *per se*. A good relationship had to be in place in order to do the work, and was seen as necessary *but not sufficient* for therapeutic change (Beck et al., 1979). Traditionally, the technical aspects of therapy have been felt to be the active ingredients. If the therapeutic relationship was a car, the cognitive therapist would use it to travel from A to B, whereas the psychodynamic or Rogerian therapist would be a collector, spending hours polishing and fine-tuning each vehicle. For many clients, particularly those whose problems are amenable to short-term counselling, a mode of transport is called for: it is sufficient for the counsellor to be warm, empathic, respectful and collaborative for the therapeutic work to proceed. However, for clients with long-term difficulties, more complex problems, personality disorders, or interpersonal difficulties, the therapeutic relationship becomes more significant (Beck et al., 1990; Safran, 1990; Safran and Segal, 1990). For these clients, because their core conflicts are often interpersonal in nature, it is likely that the therapeutic relationship will prove a rich source of information for understanding them and their difficulties. It is also likely that there will be issues and difficulties in the therapeutic relationship, and the travellers may well have to turn their hand to mechanics and body-work.

Although the 'necessary but not sufficient' view of the therapeutic relationship has been central to cognitive therapy, more attention is now being paid to the importance of the therapeutic relationship itself. It comes as no surprise that the research in cognitive therapy supports what our humanistic colleagues have been saying all along: that the quality of the relationship is central. Various studies looking at the relative contribution of non-specific, relationship factors versus technical factors in therapy indicate the importance of both, a positive relationship making a significant contribution to the outcome of cognitive therapy (Burns and Nolen-Hoeksema, 1992; DeRubeis and Feeley, 1990; Horvath, 1995; Persons, 1989; Persons and Burns, 1985; Raue and Goldfried, 1994; Wright and Davis, 1994). There is also more attention being paid to ways in which the therapeutic relationship itself can be used as an active ingredient in therapy (Beck et al., 1990; Jacobson, 1989; Safran, 1990; Safran and Segal, 1990; Young, 1994). For example, the relationship can provide an arena in which the client can practise alternatives or new behaviours, such as being angry with the therapist or expressing emotion rather than avoiding it; for clients who believe that people always let them down, the relationship in which the therapist does her best to be reliable and trustworthy can begin the process of challenging the client's beliefs.

The Core Conditions

> The general characteristics of the therapist which facilitate the application of cognitive therapy . . . include warmth, accurate empathy and genuineness. . . . [I]f these attributes are over-emphasised or applied artlessly, they may become disruptive to the therapeutic collaboration. . . . [W]e believe that these characteristics in themselves are necessary but not sufficient to produce optimum therapeutic effect. . . . [T]he techniques in this book are intended to be applied in a tactful, therapeutic and human manner by a fallible person – the therapist . . . [A] genuine therapist is honest with himself as well as with the client. (Beck et al., 1979, pp. 45–9)

The therapeutic relationship is central to cognitive therapy in many ways. It is an, often unstated, assumption that the core conditions of any therapy, namely empathy, understanding, genuineness, respect, congruence and unconditional, non-possessive positive regard (for example, Rogers, 1957) have to be in place before any therapeutic work can proceed. If the client does not feel understood, or respected, his inner world cannot be shared with another and the idea of being able to identify and challenge his strange and illogical thoughts will not get off the ground: Mr Spock constantly challenges the view of mere humans, but who wants to trust Mr Spock with their innermost secrets? Sharing thoughts and emotions can leave the client feeling vulnerable, his inner world laid open to another. Therefore, the therapist has to show the core conditions of any therapeutic relationship in order for any therapeutic encounter to proceed. Much of the importance of the therapeutic relationship has been implicit rather than explicit in cognitive therapy writings. For example, in *Cognitive Therapy and the Emotional Disorders*, Beck devotes one line to the subject: 'if the therapist shows the following characteristics, a successful outcome is facilitated: genuine warmth, acceptance, and accurate empathy' (1976, p. 221). This does not mean that Beck only paid token attention to these qualities. Throughout his work he stresses the importance of showing the client warmth, acceptance and respect, giving an impression that 'This is someone I can trust'. Listening, summarising, reflecting, reflecting feelings, and all those characteristics that make for a warm encounter are vital to cognitive therapy. Such qualities also enable the client and therapist to work together to challenge thoughts and beliefs which are problematic to the client, to enable such challenging work to take place.

It is a common observation of beginner cognitive therapists that the core conditions initially go out of the window as the therapist struggles to offer the client techniques to help identify and challenge thoughts and beliefs, somehow picking up the idea that it is more important to be a technical whiz kid than it is to be, first and foremost, a good therapist. Both go hand in hand: the tools of cognitive therapy, without the core conditions, as well as vice versa, are not sufficient for therapeutic change. The process of learning cognitive therapy involves both mastering techniques and integrating these into the context of the relationship, a process which develops as the therapist's skills increase. Cognitive therapy also allows adaptation of the core conditions to maximise their helpfulness to the individual client: for example, too much empathy or warmth may be perceived as threatening to, say, a very depressed client, who believes 'I do not deserve such caring' or 'No-one understands me, why is she pretending?' Hence the value of a good conceptualisation of the client's needs, in being able to modify the core conditions accordingly.

Going Beyond the Core Conditions: Collaboration

One important way in which cognitive therapy parts company from other forms of therapy resides in its use of conceptualisation and a collaborative therapeutic relationship. There is no doubt that cognitive therapy uses factors which are common to many other therapies. However, cognitive therapy is more specific in how such factors are used. Beck (1991), reviewing the development of cognitive therapy, states that the active ingredient of many of the 'common factors' amongst various psychotherapies, including the therapeutic relationship, is that the end result is cognitive change. Cognitive therapy aims to produce the same result but by a more direct route. 'I certainly consider the therapeutic alliance as a common factor shared with other therapies. But I also believe that the shared and explicit focus on changing belief systems, reinforcing and refining reality testing, and developing coping strategies makes for a more robust therapy' (Beck, 1991, p. 194). The way such work is achieved is by means of developing a *collaborative relationship* and *collaborative empiricism* (for example, Beck et al., 1979, 1985). In the words of Beck et al.:

> The cognitive therapist implies that there is a team approach to the solution of a patient's problem: that is, a therapeutic alliance where the patient supplies raw data (reports on thoughts and behaviour . . .) while the therapist provides structure and expertise on how to solve problems. The emphasis is on working on problems rather than on correcting defects or changing personality. The therapist fosters the attitude 'two heads are better than one' in approaching personal difficulties. When the patient is so entangled in symptoms that he is unable to join in problem solving, the therapist may have to assume a leading role. As therapy progresses, the patient is encouraged to take a more active stance. (1985, p. 175)

Collaborative empiricism helps the therapist to 'get alongside' the client, so that the work of 'attacking' the client's problems will not be seen as an attack on the client herself. In the words of Beck:

> It is useful to conceive of the patient–therapist relationship as a joint effort. It is not the therapist's function to reform the patient: rather his role is working with the patient against 'it', the patient's problem. Placing emphasis on solving problems, rather than his presumed deficits or bad habits, helps the patient to examine his difficulties with

more detachment and makes him less prone to experience shame, a sense of inferiority and defensiveness. (1976, p. 221).

What does this mean in practice? Beck et al. (1985) spell out two implications:

- *The relationship develops on a reciprocal basis.* Both therapist and client are working together to observe what is going on, to observe and comment on the client's way of being, to offer solutions to the problems and difficulties facing the client. When the client is unable to see the way forward, or is unable to see an alternative to his thoughts or beliefs, the therapist may be able to look from a different view and offer this to the client. Similarly, the client can see and offer to the therapist another perspective. There is a feeling in cognitive therapy of both client and therapist rolling up their sleeves and getting on with the work.
- *Avoid hidden agendas.* Cognitive therapy is an explicit therapy. The therapist does not form hypotheses about the client, or interpretations, and keep these to herself. Instead, everything is out on the table. If client and therapist are working to different agendas, then it is unlikely that therapy will proceed smoothly. If the therapist is trying to manoeuvre the client into seeing things from her point of view, or trying to get the client to be more logical, whilst the client simply wants to feel understood, again therapy will be a rough ride. Instead, the therapist is clear and explicit about what is in her mind, so that agendas for therapy as a whole, as well as for individual sessions and moment to moment interactions in the session, are known to both client and therapist. This means that the therapist admits mistakes, is open to suggestions, and willing to go where the client wants to go, without colluding with his difficulties.

A spirit of collaboration gives a slow, reflective 'ping-pong' quality to sessions: the time that therapist and client are speaking may be about equal; the therapist shares her thoughts about the client's thoughts, and asks for feedback. Whilst questions may be asked by both therapist and client, both work together, collaboratively and empirically, to find answers. The client's thoughts, feelings and behaviours are reflected on, not interpreted. The spirit of collaboration may be clearer when it is absent: when, for example, the therapist tells the client what to do or think; or she comes up with a brilliant suggestion about how the client may view a situation, which leaves him cold. Collaboration may also be absent when there are long silences in the session; when, rather than the silence representing a meaning-laden pause, it leaves the client high and dry, struggling with where to go next. In true collaboration, the therapist is willing to help the client out without being patronising, condescending or disempowering the client. In developing a good therapeutic collaboration, therapists should be warm, open, empathic, concerned, respectful and non-judgemental. The process of developing such a collaborative relationship involves working with the client to set goals for counselling, determine priorities, maintain a therapeutic focus and structure both within sessions and across counselling as a whole.

Using the Therapeutic Relationship in Cognitive Therapy

We have discussed in Chapter 1 how the interpersonal has been brought centre stage in cognitive therapy. Safran and Segal (1990) see a strong imperative for humans to maintain relatedness. Maintaining relatedness to others has survival value not only to the infant during his long period of dependency, but also to all people. This means that the core beliefs and assumptions that people hold about life and the world are likely to be interpersonal. In practice, clients will bring their interpersonal style, and difficulties, into therapy, as illustrated by Jane (p. 20. Such issues can be actively used in therapy.

Safran and Segal (1990) stress that the therapeutic relationship is not something that either is or is not in place for the real work of therapy to begin, but rather is a quality that continually fluctuates and which can be actively used in therapy. The concepts of transference and countertransference are far from neglected in cognitive therapy, but can and should be used as valuable aids to conceptualisation as well as to therapeutic progress. The therapeutic relationship in cognitive therapy is also actively used to work on clients' interpersonal schemata, in a way which mirrors humanistic ways of working. We examine these concepts in turn.

The Use of Transference to Aid Conceptualisation

In order for the therapist to deal effectively with his or her own role in the interaction, it is imperative that he or she have an intellectual and

*an empathic understanding of the cognitive and emotional baggage
that the patient brings to sessions. (Layden et al., 1993, p. 117)*

What goes on in the relationship can be used as valuable information to help to understand and conceptualise the client's difficulties. The client's reactions to the therapist, and the therapy, whilst
not forming the cornerstone of therapy, nor being deliberately
provoked in cognitive therapy, provide 'windows into the
patient's private world' (Beck et al., 1990). Safran and Segal
(1990; Safran, 1990) conceptualise a 'dysfunctional cognitive-
interpersonal cycle', viewing problems or ruptures in the therapeutic relationship as unique opportunities to assess clients'
beliefs.

The therapeutic relationship is an arena in which the client may
engage in a variety of schema-driven behaviours, and where
schema maintenance can be seen in action. Therefore what happens in the therapeutic relationship is very likely to mirror the
client's psychological make-up: the core beliefs and assumptions
and the mechanisms by which the client confirms these assumptions are illustrated *in vivo* (Beck et al., 1990; Persons, 1989; Safran,
1990; Safran and Segal, 1990; Wright and Davis, 1994). Persons'
case formulation approach (1989) assumes that the client's behaviour with and reaction to the therapist may be driven by her
underlying problems, and therefore is similar to behaviours with
others. For example, being late for sessions or not doing homework may be driven by a number of different schemata: schemata
relating to extremely high standards, resulting in problems with
being disorganised and chaotic outside and an inability to get
anything done on time; or to core beliefs of 'worthlessness', so
that the client does not feel it is worth making the effort for herself
to try anything that might help. Alternatively, the client may not
be willing to come to sessions on time, or work on tasks between
sessions, which may indicate fear of dependency on the therapist
or therapy. Therefore, what goes on in the client's relationship
with the therapists gives valuable clues about possible underlying
mechanisms. People who have a strong need for advice, information and reassurance about how to lead their lives will have
evolved specific, and possibly subtle, behaviours, leading the
counsellor to become a 'friendly expert', giving advice, or doing
all the work in sessions. Detecting tell-tale signs of a 'transference'
cognition uses the same means as detecting any in-session automatic thought: a sudden change in the client's emotional response
or non-verbal behaviour, such as a shift in gaze, or rapid change

of topic. Whilst it is important to note these reactions, it may not always be appropriate to work on them there and then, being too threatening for the client and risking closure of affect or risking the therapeutic collaboration.

The therapeutic relationship is affected by the processes of schema maintenance, schema avoidance and schema compensation, described by Young (1994). We actively engage in behaviours which perpetuate our beliefs – schema maintenance behaviours. In the therapeutic relationship, it is likely that clients will be testing out the therapist to check for a good 'fit' with their assumptions and beliefs, a process which the psychodynamic world describes as a 'transference test'. For example, the belief that 'I'm boring' may lead the client to speak or behave in a flat, boring manner, or selectively attend to any tiny cues that the therapist is finding them boring. Schema avoidance describes the affective, cognitive and behavioural processes employed to avoid activating schemata: for example, the client would change the subject, or laugh, whenever something painful was being approached. Schema compensation describes the process of acting in a way opposite to that predicted by the schema. For example, if the client has a 'dependence' schema (Young and Klosco, 1993), he may become very passive or dependent in the therapeutic relationship (schema maintenance); refuse to trust the therapist, or prematurely discontinue therapy, saying that he would prefer to carry on alone (schema compensation); or continually avoid talking about difficult issues, changing the subject and presenting with new crises each week (schema avoidance). All such responses may test the therapeutic relationship. Schema maintenance is illustrated in the following example.

> Tony had struggled for years with persistent abdominal pains and believed that 'No-one is to be trusted'. He compensated for his belief with an assumption that 'If I search long and hard enough, I'll be able to find the one person who can help me with my problems'. He had spent years consulting doctors, in several different countries; during which time he had also collected numerous examples of medical incompetence, as his frequent tests inevitably had their side-effects. From the start of therapy I (DS) would find myself subtly manoeuvred into situations where I did not know the answers, which proved his point. I became, inevitably, frustrated and irritated with him, and found myself feeling completely incompetent. I wanted to discharge him quickly, thereby confirming his beliefs that no-one could help him.

The client's assumptions and beliefs about relationships may force the counsellor into a 'damned if I do, damned if I don't' situation (Layden et al., 1993). This feeling is characteristic of working with clients where their experiences and resulting schemata mean that whatever others do can be misconstrued in a negative way, resulting in a 'no-win' situation in close relationships. As a response, the counsellor can also react in a black and white way. The therapist may respond to the client's outbursts and irrational demands by eagerness to end counselling and discharge the client, labelling him as 'impossible to help'. Alternatively, at the other extreme, the counsellor may become a rescuer, going to unusual extremes to help the client or offer him unrealistic assurances about her ability to help, inevitably leading him to feel disillusioned or betrayed. The therapeutic relationship may 'ping-pong' back and forward between the two extremes of over-distancing and over-involvement, mirroring the client's schema and problems. For example, a client who was sexually abused by someone she trusted learned that it was extremely difficult to trust anyone; at the same time, she learned that the only way to attain love was to be violated in some way. In therapy, the client both craved the therapist's affection and acceptance, but reacted with horror and distrust when the therapist showed signs of caring. When the therapist, in response to the patient's withdrawal, acted in a more reserved way, the client jumped to the opposite extreme, perceiving the therapist as abandoning and neglecting her (Layden et al., 1993). Layden et al. (1993), talking about clients with borderline personality disorder, stress that if the therapist has powerful, anti-therapeutic reactions to the client, this will feed into the borderline client's propensity for mistrusting the therapist. These clients may test out the therapist with a variety of 'schema-driven' behaviours. In contrast, the process of disconfirming the client's assumptions leads to therapeutic progress, so long as the disconfirmation is accepted and integrated by the client, allowing schema modification.

Countertransference and Cognitive Therapy

The classic psychoanalytic view maintains that 'countertransference' is the sum of the counsellor's reactions to the client's transference, the various feelings that are evoked in the therapist by the client (Jacobs, 1988). Various types of countertransference are described: 'classical', the counsellor's transference to the client; 'neurotic', relating to the counsellor's unresolved personal issues; 'role', the counsellor's response to the role that the client has put him in; or 'complementary', where the counsellor begins to experience what is going on for the client and is being unconsciously communicated with. In cognitive therapy, countertransference is viewed as a valuable means of gaining a deeper understanding of the therapeutic process; it represents the totality of the counsellor's responses to the client, including thoughts, schemata, emotions, actions and intentions (Layden et al., 1993). Counsellors' feelings and reactions are used 'in the service of therapy rather than allowing them to become obstacles in therapy' (Safran and Segal, 1990, p. 41), as the following illustrates.

> Alison came across as gloomy and miserable even when she was describing things that she had enjoyed at the time. I (DS) experienced her as moaning, and felt that what she said was, somehow, lacking substance. It was, for me, an almost intangible feeling of dread before the sessions, when I would find myself feeling very cheerful in contrast to her glumness. She described wanting to have a boyfriend but had difficulties in forming any relationships that lasted more than a few weeks. Inside me, a voice said 'I'm not surprised people don't stay around. Who would want such a misery guts?' Although it was not appropriate for me to feed back this to her, we looked at her feelings about relationships, and identified her tactic of having problems to gain people's attention, linked to the assumption 'I can only get love and help from others if I am really miserable: otherwise they are not interested in me'. As soon as the assumption was identified and discussed, the feeling of sessions changed, and she was able to describe a greater variety of feelings, both happy and sad. In this example, my own feelings were an accurate reflection of the client's assumption.

Much of interpersonal communication takes place at a non-verbal level: subtle posture, eye contact, tone of voice or muscle tension. Therefore it can be hard to define why the therapist is reacting in a certain way. The therapist's bodily reactions, images or metaphors can provide useful clues to the conceptualisation. I (DS) nicknamed one of my clients 'Malteser Man', because of my habit of buying maltesers after our sessions. On reflection, I realised that I perceived him as empty and sapping my energy. He filled his life with consultations to numerous doctors with his aches and pains. Having identified this feeling of emptiness, we could begin to conceptualise some of his problems in terms of beliefs around life being 'hard work', 'It's too risky to get close to anyone' and 'The only safe place is work'. Images of myself in the therapeutic relationship have provided important clues as to the client's conceptualisation. Feeling like a 'wise owl' has served me well in identifying the client's need for reassurance. If, conversely, the client believes that no-one can help, then the client may well treat the therapist with suspicion: a clue to this is if I find myself trying exceptionally hard, and against all odds, to 'sell' the model to the client with my 'estate agent' hat. Supervision is the ideal place to explore these reactions to clients, and therapists often need help and support in working out the most therapeutic responses.

The Therapist's Role in the Relationship

Cognitive therapy also looks at the influence of the therapist on the therapeutic relationship. Rather than assuming that we feel a certain way about a client because this is an effect of the client's schema, cognitive therapy looks at the effect of the therapist's schema on the therapeutic relationship. Therapists are only too human. We have our own 'blind spots and particular areas of sensitivity' which inevitably interact with the client's problems. Our schemata, assumptions and experiences lead us to act, react and feel in certain ways in therapy. Therefore, any conceptualisation of issues in the therapeutic relationship has to involve us as therapists as well as the client.

Safran and Segal (1990) stress that the therapist needs to have a sufficiently flexible, and accepting, self-concept to be able to acknowledge and accept her or his own feelings in the therapeutic interaction. It is helpful if the therapist is aware of her own rules, assumptions and schemata which may interfere with her ability to either identify or work with particular client issues or difficulties in the therapeutic relationship. Lists of common unhelpful therapist assumptions are given in Freeman et al. (1990). Assumptions such as 'It is wrong to dislike/disagree with/feel attracted to/be angry with my clients', 'I must not get angry', 'I should not dislike my client', or 'I must cure the patient' are likely to interfere with the therapeutic relationship: if the therapist has particular feelings or thoughts that contravene her rules, then they may be ignored or put back on to the client, rather than be actively used in therapy. If, for example, the therapist felt annoyed with a client, and also believed she must never show or share this annoyance, she may be more likely to think 'The client is being irritating: it is his fault: I won't let it affect me', rather than stopping and thinking what exactly is going on to arouse these feelings of annoyance in her. If the therapist has difficulty in empathising with certain feelings of the client, it may be because she cannot accept these in herself. For example, if the client is describing angry feelings towards a deceased friend, the therapist may find these feelings difficult to accept if she similarly feels rage towards someone for dying but believes 'I shouldn't be angry'. Any strong thoughts such as 'I hate working with clients who are x' indicates that the therapist may have issues that may need looking at in order to work with that client group. If the therapist is working with a relatively new problem, or if she has just learned more about a problem, the long-suffering client may receive a mini-lecture on her new-found knowledge on his particular disorder. The therapist's thoughts 'I must be shown to know something about this problem' may lead her to be over-professional and knowledgeable.

Whilst examination of our own feelings and beliefs is explicit in other therapies, cognitive therapy is beginning to pay more attention to explicit means of examining and working with our own psychological make-up. Mary Ann Layden (Layden et al., 1993), Christine Padesky and Kathleen Mooney, for example, stress the importance of cognitive therapists examining and paying attention to their own schemata, particularly when working with clients with long-term difficulties in the interpersonal arena and personality disorders, where both client's and therapist's schemata may be activated in sessions. Cognitive therapy itself provides a number of tools which therapists can use to understand their role in the therapeutic relationship, and again we stress the importance and value of supervision.

Using the Therapeutic Relationship to Produce Change

Rather than viewing difficulties in the therapeutic relationship as needing to be resolved before the real therapeutic work can start, working on these difficulties may in itself be central to the process of change. Working on the therapeutic relationship is a powerful way of working on the psychological difficulties which are the basis of the patient's problems (Persons, 1989). Young (1994) has written about how the therapeutic relationship can offer the client a form of re-parenting, where her schemata can be directly challenged in the relationship with the therapist. The therapeutic relationship can be a corrective experience in itself, particularly for clients with long-term difficulties characteristic of the personality disorders (for example, Young, 1994; Young and Klosko, 1993). Sorting out difficulties may be a means of helping clients to sort out difficulties in other relationships, providing a model for the client to solve relationship difficulties. The relationship can act as a testing ground for challenging beliefs (Jacobson, 1989). Careful self-disclosure from the therapist can offer experimental evidence for clients of the possible impact of their way of being on others in their environment. Similarly, resolving difficulties can be used as a behavioural experiment in order to test and challenge beliefs, particularly about others (Beck et al., 1990). This is illustrated with Sonja.

> Sonja would weep in sessions, about how difficult everything was, how frightened she was of never being able to cope. For many clients this would evoke empathy and understanding. However, with Sonja I (DS) would mentally walk out of the door, and feel impatient and non-empathic with her tears. I gently fed this back to Sonja, how her crying and calls for help seemed to have the opposite effect to the one she wanted, which in turn made her feel more desperate, and weep more. Her weeping, we conceptualised, was a cry for help rather than an expression of sadness. We then looked at how she might more effectively get the help she wanted, enabling her to test out my reactions to the changes in her in sessions, as well as try out different ways of behaving outside sessions. Gradually, the weeping and wailing was replaced by more genuine expressions of sadness and fear, in turn leading to a more genuine and helpful response from others. The therapeutic relationship, for Sonja, was in itself an important arena for change.

Conclusion

In conclusion, the therapeutic relationship in cognitive therapy in many ways differs little from the therapeutic relationship in other models of therapy. It is often used in a more explicit and collaborative way, and whilst not necessarily the focus of therapy, can be actively used in the service of therapy. Issues in the therapeutic relationship, transference and countertransference, are not simply problems to be solved before getting on with the real work of therapy but are sources of information about the client, and can be used to both identify and modify beliefs and assumptions. It is also important to note that the client is not the only one to benefit if we as therapists are open to the information about ourselves which is generated within the therapeutic relationship.

PART II
APPLYING THE COGNITIVE THERAPY APPROACH TO COUNSELLING

4

Beginning, Engaging and Providing a Rationale

Therapeutic counselling begins with two initial stages: the very first contact between counsellor and client, and the first meeting. Contact between client and counsellor often starts before the first full counselling session. Exactly how the first contact is made will depend on the setting in which the counsellor practises. The client may call first to make a general enquiry or to refer himself. Either client or counsellor may initiate contact after the referral system has put them into touch with each other. As this kind of contact is usually conducted on the telephone, it is often relatively brief and geared towards setting up the first face-to-face session. The first session then moves on to more formal assessment. In cognitive therapy in particular, both stages involve introducing the client to the cognitive way of working, beginning to develop a spirit of collaboration, introducing the ideas of working in a structured and focused way, and gaining feedback. These early stages also involve starting to develop a case conceptualisation.

This chapter shows how the counsellor can work cognitively from the beginning of therapy. The counsellor engages the client with a collaborative working style which emphasises the use of continuous feedback, and gives the client a clear rationale for what the therapist and the therapy is aiming to do. This cognitive style is taken into the assessment process, which aims to appraise not only the client's overall situation but also her capacity and willingness to enter into cognitive work. After the assessment phase, subsequent sessions follow a structure, which helps the client to become familiar with the therapy and consequently promotes her ability to use the therapy.

Initial Contacts: Working Collaboratively and Gaining Feedback

During initial contacts between client and therapist, working collaboratively may consist mainly of taking a very open stance towards the client – 'Is there anything, about counselling, or about me, that you'd like to ask about or discuss at this stage?' In our experience, many clients opt to wait for face-to-face contact before asking such questions. Nevertheless, the opportunity has been offered and a degree of openness established. Additionally, some clients do raise valuable and important questions at this stage. Despite some growth in public knowledge about counselling in recent years, there are still areas of ignorance and misunderstanding, raising questions such as 'Can talking really help?' and 'How long will the counselling go on?' Although it is probably best to regard these questions as requests for information, the counsellor will also be aware of starting to get glimpses into the windows of the client's world-view. Whilst these glimpses are mainly noted and put aside for another day, there may be some occasions when useful therapeutic work can be done at an early stage. The following example illustrates how a client's secondary appraisal of their problem issue, such as feeling stupid for feeling depressed, may interfere with their motivation to even get to the first face-to-face session.

> *Client*: I don't know if I'd just be wasting your time really. I sometimes think that it's all so trivial . . .
> *Counsellor*: Sometimes it seems hardly worth bothering with?
> *Client*: I'm just letting things get to me, it's so stupid. . . .
> *Counsellor*: So you *can* imagine not letting them get to you like this?
> *Client*: . . . Mmm . . . Yes, some days I can . . .
> *Counsellor*: So perhaps one thing we could work on might be getting those kind of days more often . . .
> *Client*: . . . Mmm . . . Yes [*uncertainly*] . . . it would be hard, though . . .
> *Counsellor*: Yeah, it may be hard . . . Worth giving it a go? . . . What do you think?

Beck et al. (1979) stress the importance of gathering feedback regularly, especially at the end of each session. Feedback is also a good 'marker' to end an initial contact, with questions such as 'How do you feel about the sorts of things we've discussed during our call?' or 'Was there anything I said that you didn't like?' The latter question is probably the real crux of the matter. Most of us can accept positive feedback more than readily, but we may have to do more work on ourselves to really want to know what our clients do not like about us and our therapeutic style. Yet it is crucial that we are aware of negative as well as positive reactions because negative client reactions can easily bring counselling to an abrupt halt. Therapists may often need to look at their own negative automatic thoughts ('Ungrateful sod!'), dysfunctional assumptions ('If I work hard at counselling, I will be recognised as a good therapist and wonderful human being') and maladaptive core beliefs ('I must be the perfect counsellor'), as discussed in Chapter 3.

Continuous feedback should help the therapy to stay as close as possible to the client's needs so that a kind of 'rolling contract' (Wills, in press) between therapist and client develops. Continuous feedback and the therapist's attempts to explain what she is doing by giving rationales for each move mean that the therapeutic contract will be re-negotiated regularly on an ongoing basis.

Assessment in Cognitive Therapy

A Rationale for Assessment: Counsellors' Objections
The aim of assessment is not to 'label' or 'diagnose' the client but to reach some early, and therefore provisional, agreement on the issues to be worked on in therapy. It is probably the case that all counsellors do begin to assess from a relatively early stage – yet the tradition within the cognitive approach has been to make assessment a more structured step. As Dryden and Feltham (1994) point out, structured and explicit assessment of clients carries negative connotations for some counsellors. The objections are usually that assessment can easily turn into a judgemental process with an implication that the counsellor is an expert, which is in some way out of tune with the concept of therapeutic alliance favoured by many counsellors. These objections are obviously valuable, yet seem to cut the counsellor off from a source of potentially great help to both parties in therapy. Regarding being an 'expert', it may be that some counsellors are reluctant to face

the issues raised by expertise. It has been said that the difference between counsellors and psychotherapists is that counsellors have rather more power than they think they have and psychotherapists have rather less power than they think they have.

One potentially helpful way out of this logjam might be to distinguish clearly between 'being an expert' and 'having expertise'. In our view, the client will frequently expect that the counsellor lays claim to some expertise. The counsellor can regard his expertise as expertise about people in general but that this will prove of little avail unless it can ally itself with the client's expertise about her life. This view seems consonant with the concept of 'collaborative empiricism' described by Beck et al. (1979) and elaborated by cognitive therapists such as Guidano and Liotti (1983), Persons (1989), Safran and Segal (1990), Young (1994) and Layden et al. (1993):

> The only way for therapists to accept [clients] as the final arbiters of their own reality is to be genuinely open to the possibility that the [client] knows something about reality that the therapist does not. (Safran and Segal, 1990, p. 9)

Areas Covered in Assessment

There are three main areas to cover in any initial assessment:

1 Problem-focused information (Cross-sectional).
2 Broader background information (Historical/Longitudinal).
3 Interpersonal information.

To some extent, such areas represent a coming together of three different strands within the cognitive approach: (1) the original model (Beck et al., 1979); (2) the schema-focused approach (Young, 1994); and (3) the cognitive-interpersonal approach (Safran and Segal, 1990). Different counsellors are likely to be drawn to different mixes of these models and therefore to somewhat different information gathering styles. The original cognitive model laid a lot of emphasis on gaining precise data, which, in practice, seems to sit rather more comfortably with psychiatrists and clinical psychologists than with many counsellors. Counsellors are often attracted to recent, more explorative cognitive models which lay greater emphasis on historical and interpersonal information gathering. In practice, we believe that it is important to have a balance between different ways of collecting information. Firing a lot of specific, closed questions at a client is as undesirable as getting lost in endless exploration of past experience.

---

1   Problem-focused information
    (a)   Presenting difficulties: Negative emotions, automatic
          thoughts, problematic behaviours.
    (b)   Baseline measures: Frequency, duration, intensity of
          presenting difficulties.
    (c)   Triggers: External and internal triggers to difficulties.

2   Broader background information
    Family background, life stresses, vulnerability factors.

3   Interpersonal information
    View of self, others and the world.
    Hopes and fears for therapy.

Figure 4.1   *Key areas of assessment*

The key areas of assessment are summarised in Figure 4.1.

The outline of assessment is not intended as a fixed rota for counsellors to stick to. Rather it is a series of coat hooks on which to hang information as it is assimilated. In our view, counsellors are more likely to use it in a less didactic and more 'conversational' (in the sense discussed by Hobson, 1985) style with their clients.

At the assessment stage of cognitive therapy, the development of a case conceptualisation is used to agree a common understanding about how the client's difficulties arose and what will be the appropriate strategies for working on them. The conceptualisation becomes a kind of map for understanding what has happened in the past, is happening now, and, crucially, how the future therapeutic work can begin to transcend some of the difficulties.

Assessing the Suitability of Cognitive Therapy for the Client

As cognitive therapy expands and develops to cover a wide range of clinical problems, and is being adapted for clients who need longer term therapy, so the number of clients for whom we are able to offer effective cognitive therapy increases. Therefore, the rules are expanding as to when cognitive therapy versus another therapeutic approach might be called for. This does not mean, however, that cognitive therapy is appropriate or helpful for everyone. Many of the research trials into its effectiveness have used only carefully selected clients, with a generally 'pure' form of the problem being evaluated, and therefore are not always representative of the range of difficulties our clients present with in clinical practice. However, the developments in cognitive therapy are allowing for greater flexibility in the way we work, and therefore potentially increasing the number of clients who may find cognitive therapy suits them.

Despite our enthusiasm for the effectiveness of cognitive therapy for many of our clients, it is still important to be aware of its limitations, and those clients who are unlikely to be able to use the approach. Safran and Segal (1990) and Dryden and Feltham (1992, 1994) have published separate short questionnaires for assessing a client's suitability for, respectively, short-term cognitive therapy and brief therapy. Clear indications of suitability are found if the client shows the following characteristics:

- Is able to access automatic thoughts.
- Is able to distinguish different emotions.
- Accepts responsibility for change.
- Understands the rationale for cognitive therapy.
- Is able to make a good enough relationship with the therapist.
- Is able to concentrate enough to focus on issues.
- The client's problems are not too severe.
- The client has some optimism regarding therapy.

Such criteria probably apply to most forms of therapy and should therefore be regarded as somewhat ideal. In practice, a client may already be well involved in therapy before it is realised that they do not meet such criteria. Cognitive therapy is continually being adapted for use with many different clients, some of whom would not meet the above criteria, such as those with chronic depression (Scott, 1992) or psychoses (Fowler et al., 1995). Therefore, the criteria are best regarded as positive indicators for standard cognitive therapy rather than as exclusion criteria for any type of cognitive therapy. In order to adapt cognitive therapy to meet the needs of many more client difficulties, it is vital that the practitioner is very familiar with the cognitive model; therefore, the criteria may be particularly appropriate for beginner cognitive therapists to follow closely. (For further information on the selection of clients for cognitive therapy, we recommend Padesky and

Greenberger, 1995; Safran and Segal, 1990; Safran et al., 1993; Young, 1994).

Giving a Rationale for Cognitive Therapy

There are several different ways to give a rationale for the therapy, depending in part on the client and in part on the type of problem the client is bringing to therapy. Rationale giving varies from a didactic explanation of the form and process to more organic explanations as therapy proceeds. In the didactic approach, the therapist explains the principles of cognitive therapy in a direct way – as a teacher might do with an evening class. This is particularly useful where the client has a diagnosable problem and is likely to find the possibility of a standard 'treatment' reassuring. For example, a client suffering from panic attacks may very clearly meet the 'textbook' model for both the problem and the solution. Therefore, the rationale may involve explaining the therapy in terms of aiming to help the client get her fears into perspective, and to work on different segments of the panic vicious cycle. Working with the depressed client, the therapy may be explained in terms of helping the client to break two vicious cycles contributing to the depression: low levels of activities and negative, depressed thinking. For many of these clients with 'diagnosable' problems, where more standard approaches apply, it is helpful for them to know that the problems are both recognisable and soluble using well-known formulas. In contrast, for clients with complex problems, the rationale may well need to be highly idiosyncratic and evolve as the therapy proceeds.

The rationale is undoubtedly most effective when it is pitched at situations with which the client is familiar and where the therapy is clearly seen to match his needs. The most valuable approach is to use a personal example. The therapist explores a situation which is characteristic of the client's problems, discussing in detail the specific emotions and thoughts. The personal example can be used to introduce the client to the basic cognitive model, by asking how thinking such a way might make him feel, and how feeling such a way might make him think. Such an exploration leads to a discussion of how focusing on the client's patterns of thinking might alter mood or behaviour. Leading on from a personalised example, the therapist can explore how thinking in a more helpful or rational way might affect how the client is feeling: for example, asking 'What if you were to think *x* instead of *y* in that situation?' A common example is to ask the client what he was thinking about in the waiting room or on his way to therapy. These thoughts are often rather anxiety provoking ('Will I perform well?'; 'What if he thinks I'm wasting his time?') and can be easily linked to subsequent anxious feelings and behaviour. This method is classically demonstrated in the well-known 'Richard' video tape, where Beck works with a depressed and anxious client. They begin the session with a discussion of how Richard felt whilst waiting for the session to begin.

The attempt to match therapy to the client begins right from the start as the rationale of the therapeutic approach is explained to the client. The therapist attempts to keep the rationale simple and relevant to the client's situation. Judith Beck describes the process: 'the therapist explains, illustrates . . . the cognitive model with the patient's own examples. . . . He tries to limit the explanations to just a couple of sentences at a time.' (1995, p. 36)

The client's examples are discussed and the discussion is taken into account in deciding whether the cognitive approach will be suitable for that client. In the case example below, the client, Alan, is a 39-year-old man who works for the Health Service. He refers himself because of what he describes as stress at work. Note how the client spontaneously goes into sentence completion mode, showing that he recognises himself in the description of depression, which in turn encourages the therapist to move quickly into cognitive work.

> *Therapist*: The basic idea of this is that the way we see the world, see what is happening to us, has a big influence on . . .
> *Alan*: How we feel.
> *Therapist*: Yes. There are probably different ways of seeing things and some seem to help us more than others. . . . If you're depressed, you seem to develop a kind of negative bias [*Alan*: Yes.] . . . not see some of the good things [*Alan*: Yes.] . . . and focus on the bad [*Alan*: Yes.]. Does that make any sense to you?
> *Alan*: Yes, yes . . . I would think so . . . because I feel at one time I could take the knocks a bit more, I suppose. . . . If anyone said I'd done something wrong, I used to be able to shrug it off quite easily.

The therapist recognises that the client has a sensitivity to criticism, and moves quickly into cognitive work by asking for a specific example of when Alan felt criticised. Alan described a meeting at which he'd had to present a report. He had felt very criticised and depressed and this led to taking two days off work. Reviewing the evidence of the comments that were made, however, revealed that comments had been 80 per cent neutral, 10 per cent negative and 10 per cent positive.

> *Therapist*: So there were an equal number of positive and negative comments?
>
> *Alan*: I would say so . . . but, I dunno, I seem to grasp, take hold of the negative things more.
>
> *Therapist*: Remember what we said before – that one of the features of depression is that you do over-focus on the . . .
>
> *Alan*: Negative.
>
> *Therapist*: I mean do you think it is possible that happened on this occasion?
>
> *Alan*: It's possible.
>
> *Therapist*: [*laughing*]: You're looking at me incredibly unbelievingly!
>
> *Alan*: No, no . . . it probably is what happened . . . it seemed though that they made more emphasis on the negative . . . or at least I thought they did.

In the above example, the therapist is able to bring this opening phase full circle by referring back to the original rationale – 'what we said before'. The client's final comment expresses some doubt about his appraisals – an indication that he is beginning to see them as hypotheses rather than 'facts'. This constitutes an excellent 'base camp' from which the therapeutic exploration can proceed. Although it is only a first session, Alan immediately gains some symptom relief, which helps to engage him in therapy and secure the therapeutic process (Beck et al., 1979).

By contrast, the next example offers an instance in which a laboured rationale quickly runs into the sand. The client, Beti, is 20 years old and a regular club-goer. She is feeling suicidal, following a relationship break-up which she experienced as humiliating. The therapist tries to offer her a rationale close to her experience:

> *Therapist*: If you were going to a disco with a mate and she thought, 'I've got to get off with someone tonight or it'll be a disaster', how do you think she'd be feeling as she went in?
>
> *Beti*: Nervous. She'd be worrying if she'd meet someone.
>
> *Therapist*: Yes, that's right. If you were with her and were thinking, 'I'd like to meet someone tonight . . . but if I don't, I can enjoy the music, have a laugh, whatever . . .' How would you feel?
>
> *Beti*: More relaxed. Not so worried.
>
> *Therapist*: So can you see then that the way you see things does affect how you feel about them?
>
> *Beti*: Mmmm . . .
>
> *Therapist*: And which of the two of you might stand the best chance of meeting someone, do you think?
>
> *Beti*: Well, that would depend on which of us was the best looking.

Beti attended for two more sessions during which she achieved some symptom relief but, in the therapist's estimate, little lasting attitudinal change. In retrospect, the therapist moved on too quickly from the client's uncertain response to his question about the effect of the 'way you see things'. Moving on did not allow Beti's doubts to be properly explored. The client's final comment, though showing an admirable realism, does indicate that the therapist might have to work quite hard at psychological change. Such hard work would not necessarily rule out a cognitive approach, but would suggest that a strongly individualised packaging would be needed. The therapist in this instance was perhaps not able to grasp the need for such packaging quickly enough.

There are two important points to remember about giving a rationale. The first is to keep it brief and try to follow the 'three-sentence rule' – the therapist should not say more than three sentences at any point in the dialogue and should be constantly seeking client feedback as she proceeds. The second is that client objections to the rationale should be welcomed and openly discussed in an explorative way – we want the client to be convinced within her own frame of reference, not from the power of therapist logic. By asking for and discussing feedback, the therapist starts from a basis of collaboration and empiricism.

Using a Problem List

The 'problem list' is a concept that has been taken into cognitive therapy from behavioural therapy. The list is usually developed in initial sessions as a simple list of the areas that clients feel are problematic in their lives and want to do some therapeutic work on. Dryden (1987) recommends that the list be kept in written form by both client and counsellor. It can therefore be used in reviews of progress during the course of counselling. The great strength of the problem list is that, in keeping with the parsimony of cognitive therapy, both client and therapist are clear as to the direction in which therapy is headed, and can therefore work towards those goals rather than being side-tracked by issues which later prove to be less relevant to the matter at hand. The downside of the problem list is that it may exclude exploration of those issues which later prove to be essential. Therefore, it is important to note that the list is not cast in stone, and can be added to and subtracted from.

Counsellors with a leaning towards behavioural work may well use the problem list frequently. Others may get the feeling articulated in a Paul Simon song: 'The nearer your destination, the more you keep slip-sliding away.' Counsellors from other traditions are likely to feel some discomfort at over-focusing on 'problems' and failing to identify client strengths. Such over-focusing may also hold the danger that one might be unable to pick up new themes and issues. Where a counsellor feels a strong ideological resistance to focusing on problems, it may often be useful to examine what that discomfort is about. Equally, where there is a strong tendency to focus on problems at the expense of being open to new ideas or material, it may be useful to try to detect in oneself any strong sense of discomfort with spontaneity. Thus, working with a problem list requires a balance between maintaining a structured focus and being flexible enough to move away from the defined issues into uncharted territory as and when the therapy requires. A rule of thumb is that, if the therapy seems to be moving off the defined client issues, it is important to check out with the client whether he wishes to continue in this direction, or get back to the previously defined goals.

Using Measures

Beck devised the Beck Depression Inventory (BDI) in 1961 and revised it in 1978. The BDI is a 21-item self-report inventory which assesses emotional, cognitive and physiological aspects of depression. The BDI can be found in a number of texts, such as Beck et al. (1979) and Blackburn (1987). There is also a manual giving guidelines on its use (Beck and Steer, 1987). It has been extensively tested for both its internal and external validity and has been found to correlate strongly with severe depression (Carson, 1986) and suicidal wishes (Weishaar and Beck, 1992).

The BDI is useful to cognitive therapists in a number of ways. Firstly, it gives an overall score which can be taken as a guideline to the degree of depression. Secondly, highly specific pieces of information can be quickly gained from it. For example, one question asks about suicidal thoughts, which offers a fairly easy way to get to discuss self-harm and suicide, valuable for some counsellors who find it difficult to initiate such discussion. There are also questions about specific cognitions such as guilt and physiological features, such as sleep disturbance. Many cognitive therapists would use the BDI at the start of every or most sessions with clients where depression is part of the picture. The development of the scores – usually in a downward direction, towards less severe symptoms – gives an indication of how the overall intervention is developing. Some counsellors, rather as we discussed for assessment, may find this procedure foreign or objectionable. Some may wonder initially if it is legitimate to use such measures outside the psychiatric domain to which they seem to belong. Most clients will happily go along with filling out the inventory forms which take only three or four minutes to complete. For some, it is actually helpful to have their depression contained or defined. It may help to inure them from self-blame if their symptoms are in some way legitimised. Some clients may refuse to fill out a BDI, perhaps because they fear what it will uncover (Persons, 1989). Others report a degree of dislike of the BDI – as a symbol of 'science' or of 'making me work', possibly linked to a degree of avoidance of unpleasant emotion.

There are a number of other measures for depression (Burns, 1989; Hamilton, 1960) and also for other problem areas such as anxiety (Beck, 1987; Burns, 1989), hopelessness (Beck et al., 1974a, 1974b), agoraphobia (Chambless et al., 1984), amongst others. Counsellors may, however, find simpler methods, such as merely asking a client to do a simple weekly rating out of 10 on problem areas. Similarly, counsellors can develop their own measures. For example, I (FW) wished to have a record of how a client was trying to increase her assertiveness at work. An Assertiveness at Work Scale was devised from a number of scaling questions about the sort of situations the client often found herself in. Giving it to the client to fill out every week showed how well she was succeeding over the period of the intervention.

When using such measures, it is important to be aware of both client's and therapist's expectations regarding them. When measures become a regular weekly feature of therapy, the client comes to understand more and more about their nature and purpose. She may therefore be tempted to reduce her scores to convince either her counsellor or herself that she is getting better. Clients may sometimes also exaggerate their scores in order to stay in the 'patient role' or avoid ending therapy. Sometimes there can be misunderstanding about what exactly is being measured, as the following illustrates.

Ben had a deep and regular concern that he would go mad. After months of counselling during which his BDI score plummeted, he confessed that he had been deliberately underscoring his BDI and BAI (Anxiety) because he couldn't stand the idea that he might not be getting rapidly better.

Lorna had been regularly filling out Depression and Anxiety inventories. Much of the work was centred on her concerns at work. Several weeks passed before it emerged that she considered that she was filling out the inventory with the view that it was about her mood at work, rather than her general mood, as the counsellor had assumed.

Both of these examples show that a degree of caution is warranted in the interpretation of symptom measures. Regular review of the purpose and meaning of using scores is therefore recommended.

Keeping Notes and Audio-Recording Sessions

Although it is not an assumption that we share, some counsellors regard writing down information in the client's presence as inappropriate. In line with qualities of structuring therapy and collaboration, recording sessions is an important ingredient of cognitive therapy. Keeping detailed notes, particularly at the assessment stage, is valuable for both client and therapist, helping the client to feel that his concerns are being noted and understood. As well as serving as a reminder for the therapist, we frequently give clients copies of the notes as a record of the sessions. As therapy proceeds, important points are written down for, and by, both client and therapist. Therapy notebooks are recommended for the client to keep notes and to help prevent the common scenario of key information becoming lost on scraps of paper. We always encourage clients to bring notebooks or notes along to each session, to review where therapy has got to so far and to serve as a reminder. In addition, it is very helpful to have a white-board to use during the session to illustrate the conceptualisation. A further record is for therapists to tape record all sessions and give the tape to the client to listen to for homework. We have found such tapes invaluable to the process of therapy, improving what is remembered from the session (even if it does include all the bits and pieces we wish we had not said!), as well as giving the client useful feedback. For example, a client believes she presents a very muddled account of her difficulties, and is surprised at how clearly she is able to describe them on tape; another client may learn that whilst she states that she really wants the therapist to help, the client never really listens to what the therapist is saying.

Session Structuring and Agenda-Setting

> 'Would you tell me, please, which way I ought to go from here?'
> 'That depends a good deal on where you want to get to,' said the Cat.
> 'I don't much care where . . .' said Alice.
> 'Then it doesn't matter which way you go,' said the Cat.
> '. . . so long as I get somewhere,' Alice added as an explanation.
> 'Oh, you're sure to do that,' said the Cat, 'if you only walk long enough.' (Lewis Carroll, Alice's Adventures in Wonderland)

One of the characteristic features of cognitive therapy is the structured, focused approach running throughout each session as well as for therapy as a whole. Blackburn and Davidson (1995) offer the following session format for cognitive therapy, one that seems to be widely followed in the field:

1 Review of the client's mood.
2 Set the agenda.
3 Review of the last homework assignment.
4 Session target(s).
5 Devising new homework assignments.
6 Session feedback.

Although such structuring may smack of anal-retentive quirks, it may be justified by the finding that a business-like attitude is very useful in therapy and indeed correlates with a positive outcome. Such an attitude is especially helpful in making the best use of frequently limited time. In practice, clients like the structure, especially because they are able to learn it, follow it and understand its purpose. It is easy for therapists to forget what an uncommon experience therapy is for most clients. Whilst it can sometimes be useful for therapy and therapists to be unpredictable, predictability can be a virtue for clients already struggling with unfamiliar problems and changes (Day and Sparacio, 1989).

When working in a structured way, it is very important that the client also agrees with the structure. Therefore, initial stages involve negotiating the structure, and being clear with the client exactly what session format we are following. Doing the correct work at the beginning is often conspicuous by its absence later on in therapy. Suddenly introducing agendas and homework later on can leave the client puzzled. Giving a rationale and explaining the therapy is often called 'socialising' the client into therapy. Whilst the term hints of behaviourism, such socialising may be seen as a two-way collaborative process, therapist and client learning how each other works and how each can adapt to work well with the other.

Reviewing the Client's Mood

The usual prelude to a review of the client's mood is for the client to complete a measure such as the BDI or the BAI before each therapy session. These two measures are widely used because depression and anxiety are such common problems for clients, although there are many other possibly relevant measures, some of which were discussed earlier. Scores need to be interpreted with care and should generally be matched with a client self-report, asking the client 'That's what the scores suggest. How has the last week seemed to you?' Usually the client self-report will match the score closely but sometimes not: 'Well, I know the scores have come down – but I still feel lousy, it doesn't feel better'. This material is often therapeutically valuable. One client, for example, reported that the day on which I (FW) saw him, Monday, was always his worst day. As we were working on work-related issues, this led quite nicely to a useful agenda item – how to start the working week.

Setting an Agenda

Although the structure of the session may be varied, agenda-setting is generally considered essential. The purposes of setting an agenda are to maximise the use of time in the session and to make sure certain items are covered. Agenda-setting also aids the client's memory of the session. We know that memories about specific sessions are often quite limited (Ley, 1978), and will no doubt be aggravated by therapeutic 'clutter'. Finally an agenda should help the session to begin collaboratively and maintain collaboration throughout the session.

The content of the agenda will most probably include both therapist items and client items and there can be useful dialogue on what to cover and when to cover it. One deficit of the Rogerian model is that it leads some client-centred counsellors to conclude that they have no right to raise things in sessions. This seems to us to deny the use of therapist skills to both therapist and client. Equally, however, counsellors must ensure that they do not impose too many issues that they would like to talk about. To do so would be bad cognitive therapy: it would not be collaborative and would not facilitate the process of the generalisation of therapy, that is, the client gradually learning to be his own therapist. Over the course of therapy, the client gradually takes more and more responsibility for agenda-setting.

Review of Previous Homework and the Setting of New Homework

The idea of setting 'homework' is sometimes difficult for counsellors, having overtones of being a teacher and an attendant authoritarian image. This sensitivity can be regarded as useful because it is just how certain clients will experience being set homework. The very word may awaken old memories of bad experiences in schools and/or in other authority situations. This possibility should lead the counsellor to undertake an exploratory discussion with the client about why homework may be useful.

The client's reaction to homework and the factors which prevent her from doing it can also be helpfully reviewed. It can be very de-motivating for clients when they have gone to the trouble of doing the homework and the counsellor either fails to follow it up or gives little time to it. This is why checking on the previous week's homework is included as an item on the session structure list. Equally, its inclusion later is a reminder to the therapist to set homework with reasonable discussion time remaining in the session. This helps to stop homework becoming an appendage, thrown in as the client leaves the counselling room. We have stressed the central importance of homework in cognitive therapy several times so far and will continue to do so as we progress through the process of therapy – as homework can begin to take on different aspects at different stages of therapy.

When considering what might be appropriate homework, the general rule is 'the simpler the better'. The client can, after all, ask for something more complex if the homework proves to be too simple. One regular homework task is to listen to the tape of the session. Reading is also a valuable homework task: either one of the many self-help cognitive therapy books, or a handout specific to the client's difficulties. Care should always be taken to read written material before it is given out, thinking about the client's frame of reference – sometimes a book or pamphlet may

Mike:

Reminder of the sessions: When you were a little boy, your Dad was a difficult man who drank a lot. He was violent and abusive towards your Mum and your brothers and sister. Your mum tried to look after you, but the situation was so bad that you got 'passed around' a lot to be looked after by others.

You came to believe 'I don't belong anywhere'. You didn't have consistent care, and didn't learn how to look after yourself properly or how you feel about things.

Aims for counselling: To learn how to stand on your own two feet more, instead of relying so much on your wife. Another aim is to learn to take critical comments less personally, and not to strike out, especially at your wife.

The homework for this week:

1   Spot how you feel when you are being criticised: Write it down in your notebook.

2   Try counting to five before reacting to criticism. Write down how it went – how you felt, any difficulties, etc.

3   Listen to the tape and write down important points in your notebook.

4   Remember to bring the notebook to the next session.

Figure 4.2   *Example of an individualised homework sheet*

unwittingly refer to some aspect of the client's situation which may be disturbing to them. Devising a homework sheet for the individual client is also valuable, influenced by the 'reformulation letter' concept of cognitive analytic therapy (Ryle, 1990). Figure 4.2 gives an example of a homework sheet, which includes the client's conceptualisation, goals for counselling and homework.

Session Targets
The targets for the session ('What do you want to talk about today?') constitute the main part of the session and will generally take up the majority of the time. The items which are worked on will be those already identified during the agenda-setting stage or issues which have arisen during the actual course of the session. It is not unusual for homework to become a central focus of the session. Working on the session targets is where the main skills and techniques of cognitive therapy will be brought to bear on the

identified issues. As has already been described, the direction of cognitive therapy tends to start at the symptom level ('bottom end') and works towards the underlying issues (the 'top end') as becomes necessary. Often the symptom-level work will begin with behaviourally oriented work, such as graded task assignments, and identifying and challenging negative automatic thoughts. These techniques will be described further in Chapter 5. At a later stage in therapy, underlying issues may be tackled by challenging dysfunctional assumptions and trying to modify core schemata via techniques such as continuum work and positive data logs. These techniques and skills will be described further in Chapter 6.

Session Feedback
The importance of feedback has already been discussed on page 69. Each session should end with the therapist taking feedback on the client's experience of the whole session.

Conclusion

The early stages of cognitive therapy set the scene for the process of therapy, with the therapist actively involving the client right from the start. The therapist explains both the overall aim and structure of the therapy, and the aim and structure of each technique. Each stage of the therapy is thereby properly intro-duced and negotiated with the client. Each section of therapy is reviewed, by asking for feedback from the client, feedback of what they have experienced and learned as well as on what may have 'jarred' with them. Thus, a 'rolling contract' is made with the client, aimed at helping her to learn to use the therapy in the most effective fashion. This contract is facilitated by the structuring of each session around key activities, a structure which can also be varied when flexibility is required.

5

Tools and Techniques of Cognitive Therapy

Cognitive therapy is, by reputation, a therapy characterised by the development of a large range of tools and techniques. Whilst some counsellors may view their principal tools as two comfy chairs and a box of tissues, the cognitive therapist is armed with tape recorders, pens and paper, thought diaries, activity schedules, questionnaires, and, in the case of the client with phobias, esoteric items in pots such as spiders or wasps. Perhaps the more technical aspects of cognitive therapy have led to some of the criticisms of it: that it is mechanistic, stressing tricks and techniques at the expense of emotions, concentrating on what methods to use in therapy rather than on the process.

Whilst it has been acknowledged that some of the early models of cognitive therapy stressed the verbal and rational over the role of emotion (Safran and Segal, 1990), this does not mean that the more rational, verbal and behavioural techniques of cognitive therapy should be rejected. The case conceptualisation approach in cognitive therapy, as well as more recent developments looking at the therapeutic relationship and the role of emotion, allows for a far more sophisticated approach, using a range of powerful tools of proven value to enable the client to understand and tackle his particular difficulties. A careful conceptualisation, within a collaborative therapeutic relationship, allows for mindful selection of which cognitive approaches may be of value to the particular client, bearing in mind both the evidence for problems in general, and the client's specific needs. In addition, cognitive therapy aims for the client to learn a set of new skills that can be applied to different problems, and therefore cope better with such difficulties in future.

> The goal of cognitive therapy is not simply to make our clients think differently or feel better today. Our goal as cognitive therapists is to teach our clients a process of evaluating their goals, thoughts, behaviours, and moods so that they can learn methods for improving their

lives for many years to come. . . . [W]e are not simply fixing problems but also teaching ways of finding solutions. (Padesky, 1993a, p. 12)

Cognitive therapy is frequently described as a way of providing our clients, and ourselves, with a tool kit for life.

In this chapter, we provide an overview of some of the commonly used tools in the cognitive therapist's kit, and guide the reader to sources describing the approaches in detail. We discuss how to chose specific approaches according to the client's conceptualisation, and how to use the technical and experimental approaches in cognitive therapy in a 'no-lose' way.

Matching the Technique to the Client's Conceptualisation

As well as using some approaches unique to cognitive therapy, such as the 'dysfunctional thought record', weekly activity schedules and behavioural experiments, cognitive therapy also uses a wide range of approaches from other disciplines. Beck, talking at a recent seminar in Oxford, had a succinct way of describing cognitive techniques. Paraphrasing his words, 'There is no such thing as a cognitive technique – only a cognitive framework.' Beck (1991) clarifies the principles of cognitive therapy and stresses that cognitive therapists can chose from a variety of therapeutic techniques so long as the basic principles of cognitive therapy are kept: the techniques should fit with the model of therapeutic change; should be based within the individual conceptualisation; and the principles of collaborative empiricism and guided discovery are used, within a structured session format. Beck reminds us that 'the whole of any system of psychotherapy is more than the sum of the parts' (1991, p. 196). As Judith Beck writes:

> Although cognitive strategies such as Socratic questioning and guided discovery are central to cognitive therapy, techniques from other orientations (especially behaviour therapy and Gestalt therapy) are used within a cognitive framework. The therapist selects techniques based on his case formulation and his objectives in specific sessions. (1995, p. 8)

The wide range of approaches leads to many questions about what to use at what point in therapy, and which approaches are likely to be helpful. Judith Beck also states,

> To keep the therapy focused and moving in the right direction, the therapist continually asks himself 'What is the specific problem here

and what am I trying to accomplish?' He is cognisant of the objectives in the current portion of the session, in the session as a whole, in the current stage of therapy, and in therapy as a whole. (1995, p. 284)

Bearing in mind the dangers of 'wild eclecticism' (Dryden, 1984), it is vital to keep the use of techniques within the overall conceptualisation. The most important questions therapist and client can ask themselves are 'What is the problem here?' and 'What kinds of things are likely to help?'

Much of the development of cognitive therapy techniques has evolved in response to particular clinical *problems*: for example, the use of activity scheduling and dysfunctional thought records has proved to be valuable in depression; the hyperventilation provocation test has evolved to help disconfirm clients' fears in the treatment of panic disorder. However effective the techniques may be in the treatment of particular problems *in general*, the approaches always need to be allied with the client's experience *in particular*. It is all too easy for the novice (and more experienced) cognitive therapist to systematically work through the repertoire of approaches, or chuck techniques at a problem in the hope one or other will work. A common observation of trainee cognitive therapists is that the approaches used in a particular session are based on the approaches learned the previous week. Thus, before introducing any 'trick of the trade' the therapist needs to ask 'How does using this approach fit with this person's individual conceptualisation', or 'Am I just using this because I don't know what to do next, or it's a new approach I've just learned?' This is not to say that the therapist cannot use general approaches for particular problems: for example, working through well-tried, well-recognised methods that have been shown to work with particular problems is reassuring to the client, giving the message that her problems are manageable and that a set of effective solutions are available. But the introduction and use of techniques has to be matched to the individual, and 'sold' to the individual in terms of her conceptualisation.

Using techniques in cognitive therapy raises questions about 'What happens if they don't work: won't this make the client feel even more hopeless and put him off cognitive therapy for life?' Although this can sometimes be the case, the risk of engendering hopelessness in both client and therapist highlights the importance of client–technique matching. The very depressed individual may be only too aware of negative thoughts, but be unable to even begin to look for alternatives; production of a dysfunctional thought record too early in therapy risks exacerbating the client's low mood. When working with clients with somatic problems, it is not unusual for them to report that they have no negative thoughts, just symptoms (Sanders, 1996), in which case, the introduction of thought records may put the client off what the therapist has to offer. The introduction of techniques needs, at all times, to be a 'no-lose' experiment. Any information about how the client approaches different therapeutic tasks can be valuable to the conceptualisation, aiding the identification of underlying assumptions and schemata. For example, if a client consistently agrees that filling in thought records would be useful but some-how never gets around to it, both client and therapist can collaboratively work together to identify what is going on. Does it reflect the client's fear of 'failing' at homework tasks or his belief 'Nothing will help' so why bother? Is the client agreeing with the therapist in a passive way to prove that the therapy is rubbish? In another example, a client not attempting activity scheduling, having agreed in the session that it would be useful to her, led to recognition of her belief 'I don't do things that I should do', and discussion about her hopelessness that her life seemed to be full of things she should do but resented doing. Such feelings and beliefs highlighted by the client's reactions to cognitive techniques then become the focus of therapy.

Identifying Thoughts and Feelings: The Bedrock of Cognitive Therapy

One of the most commonly used, and most well-known, ap-proaches in cognitive therapy is helping the client to identify emotions and accompanying thoughts, and to look for ways in which distorted or unhelpful thinking relates to particular emotions. This, as described in Chapter 2, provides the basis for the simple-level conceptualisation, as well as offering the client at least some initial changes in feelings. Much of the assessment and initial stages of cognitive therapy involve 'selling' the model linking the client's thoughts and feelings, and introducing the idea that feelings, behaviour or physiology change as a result of working at the level of the client's thoughts. How this is done in practice involves two stages. The first is to help the client to *verbalise* what she was feeling at a particular point, and what was going through her mind. The second stage involves encouraging the client to *keep a diary* of thoughts and feelings, which may then be used in the stage of helping her to discover alternative ways of thinking.

Identifying Emotions

A number of clients come into therapy not really sure what they might be feeling. Some may be aware of feeling bad, but cannot say more about the fine details. Others, particularly clients with anxiety or panic problems, will be feeling all sorts of physical sensations, but less aware of the emotions. One of the first steps, therefore, is to encourage the client to label feelings. Greenberger and Padesky (1995) stress that feelings can most often be described in one word: at its simplest, 'mad, bad, sad or glad'; in reality as a range of feelings: upset, shaky, scared, terrified, worried, hopeless, sad, panicky, furious, and so on. Greenberger and Padesky suggest that the client keeps a diary for a week or two, noting down changes in mood, and identifying specific emotions, described, as far as possible, in one word. A simple two-column diary may help to target and label key emotions and specific triggers (Figure 5.1).

Keeping a simple diary of moods enables the gradual introduction of the thought record, described below, and begins the process of 'distancing' from emotions in order to allow for change. Asking the client to identify feelings may well lead to thoughts: for example, asking the client who has panic attacks 'How did you feel?' may lead to the answer, 'I felt like I was going to lose control', which is more likely to be a thought, 'I'm going to lose control', than a feeling. Helping the client to distinguish between the two, and identify each accurately, is an important first step.

Identifying Negative Automatic Thoughts

The next step is to help the client to identify thoughts, particularly those associated with the particular emotions identified above. There are a number of ways of identifying negative thoughts, summarised in Figure 5.2.

Whilst we are all thinking some thoughts most of the time, they are often far from easy to identify. People often mix up thoughts and feelings, and find it very difficult to put their thoughts into words. We have seen how the question 'How did you feel about that?' may elicit thoughts; similarly asking for thoughts may lead to an expression of emotions. It is more helpful to ask 'What went through your mind' or 'Did you get an image or picture in your

Situation	How did I feel?
Example: Met friend in the street: she didn't stop to talk to me	Rejected (90%) Awful (80%) Anxious (70%)

Figure 5.1 *Diary of moods*

Key steps in identifying NATs:
    Pick a concrete example.
    Ask about feelings.
    And when you felt that, what went through your mind?
    Aim to identify specific thoughts.
    Turn questions into statements e.g. 'What do other people think?'
      becomes 'They think I'm really stupid', 'What if x should
      happen?' becomes 'If x happens, it would be a complete
      disaster'.

Sources of NATs:
    Shifts of affect in sessions or in real life.
    Predictions: What if you were to . . .?
    Role play.
    Induced imagery.
    Self-observation and self-monitoring: Thought diaries.

Figure 5.2 *Identifying negative automatic thoughts (NATs)*

mind . . .?' rather than 'What did you think?' The use of certain types of questions can help the client to clarify thoughts. Questions such as what, how, when, why and how are useful. It is important to elicit specific thoughts, in statements rather than questions: for example, the thought 'What if I couldn't cope?', when rephrased as 'If I didn't cope, it would be a complete disaster and I'd make a real fool of myself', thereby eliciting more emotion. A recent, concrete example of when the client noticed a change in moods can be used to identify specific thoughts connected to the emotion. The client can be asked about mental images or pictures to identify his thoughts: Did you get a picture in your mind of that happening? What is going on in the picture? Similarly, role playing particular situations or conversations can help the client to identify negative thoughts. A particularly powerful way of identifying specific thoughts is to use an in-session example. When the client's mood changes, or he becomes tearful or looks irritated, is a particularly useful time to ask about his thoughts.

A key point in identifying thoughts is to separate out which thoughts are most salient from the numerous thoughts buzzing around. Whilst one thought to target might be 'Something bad may happen', a more relevant thought is 'I feel like something awful is about to happen', which has greater explanatory power in terms of the emotion being experienced. For both client and therapist to target specific, emotionally laden thoughts is a skill which takes practice on both sides. The feeling of reaching a dead end, of not being where the action is, indicates that the process of thought identifying is not on course. The most useful thoughts to identify are those that are connected to emotions: so-called *hot cognitions* (Greenberger and Padesky, 1995). If the client's mood suddenly shifts, or the description of an event or problem is accompanied by emotion, then it can be useful to ask 'What went through your mind just then?' These hot cognitions are likely to carry far more meaning to the individual than those which are not connected to emotion, and may in some cases be extreme or unhelpful to the client.

Once the client is able to begin to distinguish and identify thoughts and feelings, the thought diary can be introduced. In its full form (see Figure 5.4, p. 98) the diary can appear intimidating and induce further feelings of panic and hopelessness. We have found it much more helpful to introduce the record in stages, as

Situation	How did I feel? (Rate 0–100)	What went through my mind? (Rate belief 0–100 per cent)
Met friend in the street: she didn't stop to talk to me	Rejected (90%) Awful (80%) Anxious (70%)	What have I done to offend her? I must have upset her last time we met: what did I say? I just know she must hate me (80%). I don't have any friends left (90%). I'm useless at friendships (100%).

Figure 5.3   *Diary of emotions and thoughts*

described by Greenberger and Padesky (1995). The two-column diary can be extended to three (Figure 5.3): identifying the situation, feelings and thoughts. The client can initially be encouraged to keep a record of all thoughts and then underline or highlight particular 'hot thoughts' accompanied by emotion. Here is where ratings come in very useful. The client keeps a record not only of thoughts and emotions, but of the relative strength of each, usually on a 0–100 scale. For example, in a crowded situation, an agoraphobic client may experience terror (95) and the thought 'I'm going to faint and make a fool of myself', which she believed 100 per cent. In the safety of home, she may become annoyed with her husband (20) and think 'He's an unhelpful old git', believed 60 per cent. For the purpose of helping the client to look at alternatives, the first, stronger, set of emotions and thoughts would be more useful to target, in light of the relative strength of the emotion (95 not 20) and her goal for therapy: to be able to go out without panicking.

Cognitive therapy stresses the importance of writing things down at many stages of the therapy. Keeping records is vitally important, helping the client to pin-point specific thoughts more accurately, and enabling distance to be created between the affect and cognitions. It is also valuable in recording specific predictions the client may be making, such as 'They'll think I'm stupid', or 'It'll be a disaster', in order to test out the predictions more accurately. We have found in practice that clients may be reluctant to write down their thoughts, believing that the act of recording what is going on will make the feelings worse, or preferring to avoid rather than focus on the thoughts. In this case, the client can be encouraged to try an experiment to test out whether keeping records does in fact make her feel worse, or whether, as is more common, writing down her thoughts enables her to begin to get them into perspective.

Modifying Negative Thoughts

Once specific negative thoughts are identified, client and counsellor can work together to test out the validity of their way of thinking, treating the thoughts or negative predictions as hypotheses to be tested rather than facts. Such an approach is named 'collaborative empiricism', using guided discovery and experiments to test out thoughts and beliefs and explore alternatives. Exploring the link between events and our interpretation must be done in a friendly and understanding way, and not give the message that there is a 'right' or 'wrong' way of seeing things, just that there are many alternatives which may influence our reactions.

It is vital to be empathic and non-judgemental; putting the thoughts into context is particularly important: 'Given your experience, it makes sense that you keep saying x to yourself.' Regular summaries can help to check that the client and counsellor are on the same wave-length. The overall message in challenging the client's way of thinking is to enable the client to take her thoughts to court, enabling information and evidence to be collected for the defence and the prosecution, rather than automatically jumping to conclusions based on one way of seeing things.

There are three main approaches to challenging thoughts: the process of guided discovery using Socratic questions; thought diaries; and behavioural experiments.

Guided Discovery and Socratic Questions
Guided discovery is an investigative process whereby client and counsellor work together in a collaborative way to see if there is a different way of seeing things. It involves asking questions in order to understand the client's point of view and help the client to discover alternatives (Beck and Young, 1985). The key method of guided discovery is the *Socratic method* which uses systematic questioning and inductive reasoning (Overholser, 1993a, 1993b).

> The goal of the Socratic method is to cultivate abstract conceptual skills. . . . Often the focus is on helping the client to derive a universally applicable definition of an abstract concept relevant to therapy (e.g. love, trust, success, friendship). Throughout this process, the therapist and client collaborate in the search for knowledge and definitions. Both therapist and client attempt to minimise their pre-conceived beliefs in order to remain cautious and sceptical about the information they possess. . . . Inductive reasoning is used to draw general inferences from experiences with specific events and therefore can . . . help clients distinguish between facts, beliefs and opinions. (Overholser, 1993b, p. 75)

The aim of the Socratic method is to guide discovery (Padesky, 1993a). Reading cognitive therapy vignettes often gives the impression that the therapist knows the answer to a particular issue, and is asking questions that lead the client to this answer. However, 'In the best cognitive therapy, there is no answer. There are only good questions that guide discovery of a million different individual answers. . . . [W]e can ask questions which either imply there is one truth the client is missing or which capture the excitement of true discovery' (Padesky, 1993a, p. 11).

The Socratic method is not a case of the counsellor trying to persuade the client to see things from his point of view. One common mistake is to ask too many leading questions, too soon, without taking time to explore why the client thinks the way he does. Questions such as 'Don't you think it would be more helpful if you did x?' or 'Do you think this way because of . . . [counsellor guesses]?' may well close down the process of discovery, impos-ing the counsellor's way of seeing before discovering the client's viewpoint. Instead, open questions, in a gentle and friendly manner, enable client and counsellor to explore issues collabor-atively. A useful question when wanting to clarify meanings is to ask 'What do you mean when you say x?' This helps to define more clearly the meaning of a thought, which may be very idiosyncratic. Other useful questions are as follows:

- What is the evidence that x is true? What is the evidence against x being true?
- What might be the worst that could happen?
- And if that happened, what then?
- What leads you to think that might happen?
- How does thinking that make you feel?
- How would that work in your body?
- Is there any other way of seeing the situation?
- What might you tell a friend to do in this situation?
- Is there something else you could say to yourself that might be more helpful?
- What do you think you could change to make things better for you?

Padesky (1993a) defines a number of characteristics of good Socratic questions. Firstly, they are those to which the client has the answer. 'Why do you think that way?' is likely to elicit 'I don't know, I just do'. 'What might be the consequences of thinking x to yourself' is more likely to elicit a useful answer, such as 'It makes me feel bad, it stops me getting on with my work'. Secondly, Socratic questioning draws the client's attention to relevant information which may be outside the client's focus. For example, the therapist might ask a client who is afraid of collapsing during a panic attack, 'When you say you're terrified that you might faint when you feel so panicky, have you ever felt really faint but not actually fainted?' The question can help the client think about the realities of fainting, moving from a vague fear to remembering information which may be useful. He may answer, 'I've felt really awful lots of times, but I've never actually collapsed . . .'. The questions can then move to discovering why this might be so: 'How might you have stopped yourself fainting?; 'If you feel faint, but don't actually collapse, what does this tell you?' Thirdly, Socratic questioning moves from the concrete to the more abstract, enabling the client to generalise from the discussion and therefore apply new information elsewhere. If the client reports being 'bad', what does this mean? Initial questions focus on specific, concrete examples or areas where the client believes himself to be 'bad', such as bad at a job, bad to be so angry. Guided discovery will initially aim to explore the meaning and relevance of badness to these examples. For example, the client may discover that he is not particularly good at some aspects of his job, but generally does a good job; whilst being angry all the time is not particularly helpful, being angry sometimes does not make him a bad person. The discussion then aims to help the client move from concrete examples to the more abstract general concept of badness. Padesky stresses the importance of asking *synthesising* questions to help the client to draw conclusions, such as 'How does this fit with what we're saying about you being a bad person?' In the above example, the client is asked to think about how the information that he is good at some parts of his job, and is not angry all the time, fits with his general belief 'I am a bad person'.

The aim of guided discovery is for the client to learn how to question thoughts and beliefs himself. Rather than just asking questions in sessions, the therapist can teach the client the kinds of question to ask in order to look for alternatives. Therefore when the client has the automatic thought 'I'm bad', he learns to ask himself 'What does bad mean?', 'What is the evidence I'm bad?', 'Is there anything in myself that is not all bad? – Why am I ignoring this at the moment?', and other questions to reduce the potency of the negative thought.

Diary of Negative Thoughts and Alternatives

Once the client has began to question her thoughts, and see that there might be alternatives, it is useful to record these using a full diary, sometimes known as a 'Dysfunctional Thought Record' or the more friendly 'thought diary'. The type of diary is shown in Figure 5.4 (Beck et al., 1979). The client will already have become proficient in recording emotions and thoughts; the last column enables her to think about and record alternative thoughts which lead to an improvement in emotion.

At first sight, the thought diary can look very complex. It is important to introduce it in stages, as described above, and adapt it to the client's needs. For example, some clients prefer to keep notebooks recording thoughts and alternatives; some may find writing down too difficult, and use the diary as a reminder to look for alternatives in their head. It is a sobering lesson for all trainee cognitive therapists to use it themselves for a period of weeks. Many of the problems faced, such as forgetting to do the diary, not wanting to identify thoughts, not being able to see alternatives, or the frequent excuse of the diary being lost or thrown away, are exactly those faced by our clients, who may also be wrestling with anxiety or depression. Therefore, the key is sensitive use, offering

Date	Situation	Emotion: How did you feel? How bad was it (0–100)?	Automatic Thoughts: What went through your mind? How much did you believe each thought (0–100)?	Alternatives to Automatic Thoughts: How much do you believe each alternative thought?	Results: 1 How much do you now believe ATs? 2 How do you feel? 3 What can you do?
Monday	Met friend in the street: she didn't stop to talk to me	Rejected (90%) Awful (80%) Anxious (70%)	What have I done to offend her? I must have upset her last time we met: what did I say? I just know she must hate me (80%). I don't have any friends left (90%). I'm useless at friendships (100%)	Just because she didn't stop, does not mean I have no friends. There may have been other reasons for her not to stop – She looked in a hurry. Chris and Ann both came over to talk to me in the coffee break today: I do have friends (60%).	1 30% 2 I feel better: less rejected, although it still hurt. 3 Say hello to her and find out if she is OK. Concentrate on people who are my friends.

Figure 5.4 *Thought diary (Beck et al., 1979)*

a good rationale for doing the diaries and spending time on the client's difficulties. Eventually, the contents of the diary become automatic thought processes; but for a period, at least, keeping the diary can be a crucial stage in helping clients to identify and challenge thoughts.

Behavioural Experiments

A behavioural experiment aims to help the client to test out thoughts and beliefs in order to discover their relative validity or truth (Beck et al., 1979). In sessions, the client may come to see that the likelihood of some terrible catastrophe occurring should he become anxious is in fact exaggerated; but will not totally believe this until it is put to the test. Two clinical examples will illustrate the use of experiments.

> Alice believed that if she was to say anything positive about herself, she would become conceited, selfish, full of herself and 'puffed up like a self-satisfied chicken'. This view was firmly entrenched in both Alice and her family, who never gave praise and whose motto was 'spare the rod and spoil the child'. Alice and I (DS) worked out an experiment for her to do over one week. Every time something went right, or she was pleased with herself (a response that she successfully repressed), or someone praised her, she had to write it down in a diary and repeat it to herself. Her hypothesis was that, by the end of the week, she would have turned into the 'self-satisfied, puffed-up chicken' that she most feared. She did her best to try to praise herself, not an easy task, and came back to the session the next week to report that she had not felt self-satisfied, more that she could begin to feel a bit better about herself, as well as better about other people. She had begun to praise other people, and noticed how they 'lit up': no-one became self-satisfied, only a bit more self-accepting. It was clear to both of us, too, that she had not turned into a chicken.

> Matthew had a terror of wasps. He believed that when he encountered a wasp, it would immediately make a 'bee line' for him, and take out its total aggression on him. He stopped this happening by running away, flapping his arms, screaming and totally avoiding, as far as possible, going outdoors during the wasp season. I (DS) spent some time exploring his beliefs that wasps single him out, and that they were hostile and aggressive without reason. We discussed how useful it was to a wasp, from an evolutionary perspective, to try to avoid creatures that are obviously bigger and more dangerous than they, rather than deliberately attacking them, and how most angry behaviour from wasps was in self-defence. Whilst Matthew agreed, in principle, with this argument, he still did not believe that wasps were at all benign. The experiment for Matthew, after some weeks of preparation, was to meet up with a wasp, but stop himself from flapping and running, and observe the

wasp's behaviour. He noticed that the wasp did mind its own business, was more interested in looking for sugar than in unleashing its fury on him, and was more likely to pay attention to him when he was afraid that when he was relaxed. From this experiment he concluded that his beliefs about wasps were exaggerated, and partly caused by his reactions to wasps rather than anything inherent in the wasp's make-up.

Other forms of disconfirmation are used in panic disorder and social phobias. For example, people who panic frequently believe that if they did not sit down, relax, breathe deeply and otherwise try to control the panic, they would faint, pass out or make a fool of themselves (Salkovskis, 1991, 1996). Therapy involves working with the client to disconfirm what he most fears. For example by going into a public place and deliberately hyperventilating in order to induce panic, and then stopping himself from sitting down, the client can see whether it is possible to pass out. Disconfirming the fear has a powerful effect on the individual's beliefs.

Behavioural experiments involve creativity on the part of both therapist and client. From our own clinical experience, we have accompanied clients into shops where they have tried to have a panic attack and faint; asked our clients who worry about their thoughts being true to worry for a week that their therapist has won the lottery in order to test out whether their thoughts do indeed have magical powers; and asked clients to conduct a survey of their friends to find out if the client is the only person who ever gets anxious in social situations. Behavioural experiments have one important pre-condition: they must be no-lose experiments, aimed at both gathering information and testing out alternatives. Whatever the outcome, something has been learned. It is preferable that the outcome will not be as the client fears, although if it is, this can also be used as an opportunity to assess whether her fears were exaggerated, or how she can learn to deal with difficult situations.

Behavioural Approaches and Cognitive Therapy

Cognitive therapy uses a range of what might be described as behavioural approaches. Many of these have evolved from the behavioural roots of cognitive therapy and are valuable in two ways. Firstly, behavioural approaches in themselves produce relief of symptoms of depression and anxiety, and give the client a means of coping with problems. Secondly, behavioural approaches can be used in the service of cognitive therapy. For example, relaxation is traditionally used for anxiety. Muscular relaxation and slow controlled breathing do relieve the physical symptoms of anxiety and therefore help the client to feel better. However, in itself, relaxation may be counterproductive. If the client believes 'Anxiety is dangerous; it may mean I faint and make a fool of myself', then he may use relaxation techniques as a form of 'safety behaviour' (Salkovskis, 1991, 1996) in order to prevent any catastrophe from happening. In which case, learning to control the symptoms has to be secondary to cognitive changes, helping the client to more realistically appraise how dangerous anxiety really is. If, however, the client believes that 'I mustn't relax – if I slowed down I'd get nothing done and become a complete cabbage', then relaxation techniques can be used to help him test out whether a relaxed approach to life does equate with inertia. In this way, careful matching of behavioural approaches to a specific understanding of the client's conceptualisation enables techniques to be used as powerful methods of change.

Weekly Activity Schedule
The weekly activity schedule is frequently used in cognitive therapy for depression, helping the client to become more active and increase the level of enjoyable activities in life (Fennell, 1989). It is a diary of a week, which the client can use to either fill in what she has been doing each day, or plan for the next day's activities (Figure 5.5). The diary also involves ratings of how enjoyable each activity was, and how much it gave the client a sense of achievement, so-called 'pleasure' and 'mastery' ratings. Planning activities in advance is a powerful means of overcoming the inertia and lack of motivation associated with depression. The weekly activity schedule can be used as a means of testing out clients' beliefs. For example, the ratings of mastery and pleasure enable the client to see how much of a sense of achievement she feels in her life; how she predicts not enjoying anything but finds out that she did gain some enjoyment after all.

Distraction
Distraction is a means of taking the mind off problems or symptoms, and paying attention to something else. It can involve physical activity, focusing on a mental image and mental 'chewing gum' such as arithmetic or remembering names of capital cities.

	Monday	Tuesday	Wednesday	Thursday	Friday	Saturday	Sunday
9–10							
10–11							
11–12							
12–1							
1–2							
2–3							
3–4							
4–5							
5–6							
6–7							
7–8							
8–12							

Figure 5.5   *Weekly activity schedule (Beck et al. 1979)*

Distraction can be very helpful to clients who are depressed, encouraging them to stop focusing on how bad they feel and focus, instead, on a practical task or activity. It can help clients to stop paying attention to anxiety, which helps the physical symptoms to reduce. For obsessional clients who ruminate about their thoughts, distraction is a means of helping them to pay attention to something other than what is going through their minds. It is also useful for clients who find it difficult to tolerate strong emotions, giving them a first aid measure, for use within sessions or in daily life, to reduce emotion when it threatens to overwhelm them.

Whilst it sounds a very simple thing to do, in practice not focusing on what might feel like overwhelming problems, emotions or issues can be very difficult. Asking the client to distract from her worries may imply that the therapist is not taking her problems seriously: therefore it is important that the client really understands the rationale behind distraction. For people who ruminate on their worries, not focusing on thoughts can initially be very anxiety provoking. Again, conceptualising the problems and solutions is important. Distraction may be used as a 'safety behaviour' related to the belief 'If I don't think about it, it won't happen and so catastrophe will be averted'. For example, people who are anxious may believe that if they paid attention to their anxious feelings, these would overwhelm them, and therefore use distraction as a means of preventing catastrophe. In this case, it is more helpful for the individual to learn that anxious feelings, whilst extremely unpleasant, are not catastrophic (Salkovskis et al., 1996). Distraction may also be a way of avoiding emotion, or for the client to avoid thinking through his negative thoughts. We therefore tend to see distraction as a means of first aid rather than a long-term solution to issues.

Problem Solving

Problem solving is a means of identifying problems and looking for feasible solutions. It has been shown to be helpful for people with depression, enabling them to look for solutions to the issues which may underlie and maintain depression (Gath and Mynors-Wallis, 1996). Problem solving encourages the client to work out practical and psychological ways of dealing with problems, using her own skills and resources as well as help from others. It can be particularly helpful for individuals where life stresses are contributing to their problems, and where the individual is either

- **Identifying and clarifying the problem:** Client and counsellor work together to identify exactly what the problem is, and other questions such as: Who is affected? What are the components of a problem? When do I need to do something about it?

- **Setting clear goals:** The client identifies what exactly she or he wants to achieve, and by when.

- **Generating a range of solutions:** Client and counsellor brainstorm what solutions might be possible. The client can also ask others for possible ideas about solutions to the problem.

- **Evaluating the solutions:** The client looks at the list of possible solutions and identifies which ones might be helpful and which can be rejected.

- **Selecting the preferred solutions:** The client ranks the solutions in order of feasibility and selects one or two to try.

- **Trying it out and evaluating progress:** The client tries out the selected solution and then thinks about how successful it was. If the solution was not helpful, the client picks another solution and puts this into practice.

Figure 5.6   *Problem solving exercise*

finding difficulty in addressing or solving these problems or avoiding tackling the problems. The stages of problem solving are shown in Figure 5.6.

Working with Assumptions: Getting to the Heart of the Problems

So far, we have looked at ways of enabling our clients to examine their patterns of thinking and behaviour, and use these to, hopefully, feel better. Often, such work in itself is helpful. However, there is usually more going on than meets the eye, and in order to produce lasting change, it is important to look at the client's way of viewing himself, others and the world. The cognitive model makes a distinction between automatic thoughts and underlying assumptions and beliefs or schemata. We look in greater detail at schemata in Chapter 6; here, we go on to examine how cognitive therapy tackles assumptions, the rules that determine how we are in the world, which may be adaptive, or contribute to ongoing difficulties. Although, on paper, cognitive therapy recommends starting at the automatic thought level and working down to assumptions, then progressing to schemata, in practice working with thoughts and assumptions often proceeds hand in hand, thoughts being the embodiment of the assumptions, sometimes in shorthand form, sometimes word for word. Therefore, the therapy may well work on both levels simultaneously.

Key Issues and Skills in Working with Assumptions

Identifying and working with clients' assumptions is helpful for a number of reasons. As we have described in Chapter 2, the cognitive model specifies the centrality of assumptions and beliefs in the development and maintenance of psychological difficulties, hence directly targeting these is vital to enable the client to change. Unhelpful assumptions leave the client vulnerable to the risk of relapse: although therapy may help her deal with and work through the present episode of the problem, unless the rules underlying the problem are also worked through, she may experience similar problems in future. Working with assumptions helps the client to develop skills to deal with future problems.

Whilst understanding the client's frame of reference is central to many different schools of counselling, cognitive therapy provides approaches that directly target the individual's way of being, thus enabling both understanding and refinement or change in the most parsimonious way. When working with assumptions and core beliefs from the perspective of cognitive therapy, many of the counselling skills used are the same as those employed in many psychotherapies. Cognitive therapy in particular emphasises working in a way that is explicit and collaborative: the client's rules are openly described, verbalised and examined as though they are hypotheses about the world rather than absolute rules (Beck et al., 1990; Young, 1994; Young and Klosco, 1993). Work with assumptions and beliefs requires a number of key skills and approaches. Despite all the drawbacks and difficulties our set of rules may pose, our assumptions and beliefs are very central to our frame of reference, fitting like a comfortable old pair of slippers. They feel right, and to act or think against them may seem dangerous and anxiety provoking. It can, therefore, be very threatening to have these beliefs exposed or challenged, and can imply to the client that they have 'got it wrong', sometimes for many years. Therefore the counsellor needs to proceed with empathy and sensitivity and work with, not against, the client. There should be no sense that some beliefs are 'right' and others are 'wrong', or a sense of the client and counsellor getting into an argument: the counsellor's task is to understand the client's viewpoint, however much the counsellor may disagree with it or see it as irrational. Should there be a sense of counsellor and client arguing against each other, the focus should become the counselling process, not the relative merits of each view. The counsellor must work at the client's own pace and be sensitive to cues, spoken or unspoken, that the client is uncomfortable with the process of counselling.

Of vital importance is for us to remind ourselves of cultural differences in assumptions: our own set of assumptions may differ significantly from those clients from different cultures, stressing the importance of understanding and working within the client's frame of reference (Alarcón and Foulks, 1995; Hays, 1995; Padesky and Greenberger, 1995). Padesky and Greenberger quote examples of how easily therapists from one culture can misinterpret and misdiagnose those from other cultures by accepting the therapist's cultural norms as healthy, and diagnosing other standards as evidence of emotional problems or personality disorders. Hence the importance of not making assumptions when working with assumptions.

Identifying Assumptions and Beliefs
The information for identifying a client's beliefs and assumptions comes from many sources (Fennell, 1989):

- Themes which emerge during counselling.
- Patterns in the client's way of thinking.
- Labelling the self or others.
- Highs or lows of mood.
- The client's response to therapy.

The process of guided discovery is a key way in which a client's assumptions are clarified. Asking questions, being curious, finding out how the client thinks and what makes him think that way enables rules to be made explicit. Rather than accepting the client's thought at face value, guided discovery enables probing to understand the underlying mechanisms. Rather than saying, with empathy, 'Yes, that would be terrible' or 'It sounds like you're very scared of that happening' when a client is talking about the fear of fainting when feeling anxious, the therapist's mode of enquiry is along the lines of 'What if that did happen . . . what would that mean?' The therapist pursues this form of questioning until it is clear that a rule is being reached, a process called the downward arrow technique (Burns, 1980). This shows the technique already described on p. 46 in use in another client situation. The downward arrow approach involves peeling away the layers of meaning to identify what is beneath the client's specific fears, the questions being repeated several times until a 'bottom line' is reached. The aim is to arrive at a statement which makes sense of the client's fears: 'If I believed *x*, then I would feel the same way.' The process is illustrated with Claudia, an adult education tutor, describing her terror of having a panic attack in front of her class.

> *Claudia*: [*Describing a recent attack*] I felt really faint: I just knew I was going to pass out.
> *Therapist*: Suppose that really happened, that you did faint . . . what would be bad about that for you?
> *Claudia*: Well, I'd fall over in front of all these people.
> *Therapist*: And suppose you did fall over: what next? What is the worst that could happen?
> *Claudia*: Well, I'd just be lying there like a complete fool . . .
> *Therapist*: Suppose what you say did happen: what would that mean to you?
> *Claudia*: It would mean I'm really out of control: just not as good as others: I can't even stand up and do my job without making a complete mess up.
> *Therapist*: And if that were true, what would that mean?
> *Claudia*: It would just show what a fake I am.
> *Therapist*: Is this something that keeps coming back to you: some form of rule?
> *Claudia*: I guess I have to be in control: If I'm not in control, people will see me for what I am: a fake.

USING IMAGERY TO IDENTIFY ASSUMPTIONS   Verbal discussion cannot always reach assumptions or rules, particularly when the assumptions are charged with emotion, or if the individual has an intellectualising style or avoids emotion by excessive talking. Working with the client's images can be a powerful way of identifying meanings to the individual (Edwards, 1990; Wells and Hackmann, 1993). Images are often far more charged with meaning than are words, and therefore give more clues as to underlying assumptions.

Ways of getting in touch with images include asking: 'Did you have a picture in your mind just then?' Once the individual has come up with an image, the client can be asked to describe it in greater detail. Questions such as 'What is happening? Who else is in the image? What are they doing or saying?' can help the client

- What is so bad about the events in the image?

- What does that mean to you?

- What is the worst that can happen?

- How do you feel right now, emotionally and in terms of body sensations in the image?

- How did you get into this situation?

- What is going through your mind in the image right now?

- Does the image remind you of anything? What are your earliest memories of the feelings/thoughts/sensations/experiences in the image? Where were you? How old were you? What was happening in your life at the time? How did you feel about yourself at that time? What does that mean?

Figure 5.7   *Questions with which to explore imagery (Wells and Hackmann, 1993)*

to be more specific about the image. Once the image is identified, the types of questions shown in Figure 5.7 can be used to help the client to unpack the image and explore its personal meaning, implications and origins.

Modifying and Revising Assumptions
Simply identifying the rules enables some clients to begin to change. Once articulated, the client may well be able to see that it is not realistic or helpful to hold such extreme black and white views. The counsellor can encourage the client to look at the grey area between the black and white extremes posed by the assumption. The assumption may be seen to be an ideal, or a preference, rather than an absolute necessity.

The process of working with assumptions is, in many ways, similar to the approaches described above to challenge thoughts: the overall aim is for the client to empirically test the assumptions, to find out the relative 'truth', helpfulness or unhelpfulness of the rules, and, if found not to measure up, to come up with alternatives. Guided discovery, Socratic questions, diaries of negative thoughts and behavioural experiments all enable more information to be gathered about the client's assumptions in order to test out their validity. Some key questions that can help to guide the client towards alternatives are shown in Figure 5.8.

- What is the assumption? What are my exact words to describe the rule?

- In what way has this rule affected me? What areas of life has it affected? e.g. school, work, relationships, leisure, domestic life?

- Where did the rule come from? What experiences contributed to its development? Rules make a lot of sense when first developed, but may need revision in the light of subsequent, or adult, experience.

- What are its pros and cons? What would I risk if I gave it up?

- In what ways is the rule unreasonable? In what ways is it a distortion of reality? What are the ways it is helping or hindering me?

- What would be a more helpful and realistic alternative, which would give me the pay-off and avoid the disadvantages? Is there another way of seeing things which is more flexible, more realistic and more helpful, giving me the advantages of the assumption without the costs?

- What do I need to do to change the rule?

Figure 5.8   *Questions to help the client discover alternative assumptions (Beck et al., 1979, 1985; Burns, 1980)*

USING IMAGES TO MODIFY ASSUMPTIONS   Clients who are able to 'think in pictures' and who are able to work with such images may find it helpful to use imagery to modify their assumptions. Although several texts on visualisation suggest that substituting a positive ending is a means of changing images, in cognitive terms this may be counterproductive since merely looking at a 'happy ending' enables the client to avoid looking at the feared catastrophes or consequences of the image, and may actually prevent her from re-evaluating the image and coming up with a more appropriate alternative. Very often people freeze the image in time and do not look beyond. Being able to examine the image may help the client to modify it, by projecting the image in time, or by re-evaluating the reality of the image. The image can help the client to experience and work with the salient emotions, facilitating cognitive and emotional processing (Foa and Kozak, 1986). Ways of working with images are described by Edwards (1990). In the example of Claudia above, she could only see complete catastrophe arising from her fainting in front of the class: being out of control and seen as a fake. Once she looked at her image and projected it forward in time, she could see that people would see that she was unwell and help her, and that they would not think she was 'out of control', or judge her, for fainting.

CHALLENGING ASSUMPTIONS: TAKING RISKS   One powerful way of testing out rules is to devise experiments in which the individual does not act in accordance with the rule, but behaves as though a different rule is in operation, and tests out the consequences. For example, Claudia believed, 'I must be in control all the time: if I'm not it'll prove I'm a fake'. An experiment might be for her to practise being slightly less 'in control' at work, occasionally preparing her lessons slightly less thoroughly than usual, leaving something in the staff room and having to go and get it during a class, or feeling ill in class and having to sit down, to test out whether this proved that she was 'a fake'.

It is extremely important for any experiments that the client and therapist negotiate to be no-lose situations. Whatever the outcome of the experiment, the client must be able to learn something useful. Taking risks is, by definition, threatening to the client; therefore the client needs to be supported in the decision to try something new, with a good outcome whatever happens.

Standard Cognitive Therapy and Clients with Personality Problems

There has been some question as to whether standard cognitive therapy approaches described in this chapter can help those people who also have long-term personality disorders. What use is it trying to identify and challenge negative views of the self if the client has a life-long overriding theme of the self as bad, and cannot even begin to see that there may be an alternative? Standard cognitive therapy may well be valuable in two ways. Firstly, whilst the evidence is contradictory, there is some research evidence that shows that helping clients with problems such as depression and anxiety is effective for those clients who stay in therapy, regardless of whether they also can be diagnosed as having a personality disorder (Van Nelzen and Emmelkamp, 1996). One problem in working with clients with personality problems is that they are more likely to drop out of therapy unless the approach is carefully adapted. Mary Ann Layden and others stress the importance of offering the client with borderline personality disorder a means to begin to reduce symptoms, at least in the short term, in order to begin to do the work necessary for longer-term changes (Layden et al., 1993). For example, the standard techniques can be used for the client to reduce emotions which may threaten to overwhelm the therapy process, or to alleviate depression or anxiety sufficiently to begin to work at the level of schemata. Secondly, given that the approaches in cognitive therapy are common-sense, practical, accessible and written down, we have often found that clients may not be able to make use of them during therapy, but may return to them at a later stage. For example, a client may comment at the end of therapy: 'You've shown me that there are some ways of tackling my problems. Although I've not been able to make use of them just now, I know they're something I can come back to.' Basic cognitive skills such as monitoring and challenging thoughts, behavioural experiments or problem solving form the basis of schema-focused work described in the following chapter. Therefore, if the client begins to take on board such approaches, and practise them on relatively less threatening issues, he can begin to apply the same approaches to working with core beliefs and schemata.

Conclusion

The tools and techniques of cognitive therapy are many and varied, some unique to cognitive approaches, some borrowed from other disciplines, including behaviour therapy and Gestalt therapy. We have stressed, however, that cognitive therapy, whilst using such techniques, is more than the sum of its parts, and must always be integrated with the cognitive conceptualisation within a good therapeutic relationship. The overall aim of any technique in cognitive therapy is to target and modify the client's belief systems, a process which is guided by the client's individual conceptualisation, which provides a sound understanding of what that belief system is, where it came from and how it works in practice. Thus, cognitive therapy becomes a dynamic therapy soundly based on an individual formulation, rather than a set of self-help techniques. In the words of Weishaar, 'Cognitive Therapy, viewed as a set of techniques, is not likely to be successful in treating the range of disorders confronting clinicians. Yet,

Cognitive Therapy based in a theoretical framework, grounded in psychological literature, and presented within a sustaining therapeutic relationship has wide ranging utility' (1993, p. 27). If we are tempted to simply utilise techniques, we are missing the key ingredients.

6

Themes and Patterns in Cognitive Therapy: From Personality Disorder to Schemata

Counsellors and therapists have traditionally distinguished between the 'presenting issues' and the 'underlying issues' in clients' presentations. Implicit in the idea of the underlying issue is the suggestion that the client's personality has organised around certain key themes which make them predisposed to further problems even if the current symptoms clear up. Psychiatric diagnostic systems such as the *DSM-IV* (the fourth edition of the *Diagnostic and Statistical Manual* published periodically since the 1960s by the American Psychiatric Association) have used the term 'personality disorder' to describe this phenomenon. The term 'personality disorder' is one to which many counsellors would react most negatively. For us, however, the concepts underlying the term have proved invaluable, if not a quantum leap in our practice. The purpose of this chapter is to unpack the issues of the label 'personality disorder' and to present them in a user-friendly way. We aim to help counsellors to put away their immediate reaction to the term and rethink the concept's usefulness to them – again an empirical approach which is congruent with the general values of cognitive therapy. It may well be that, like us, you will find the concept useful but want to throw away the term.

Personality Disorders

The term 'personality disorder' is a relatively recent one. It was first used in the *DSM* in 1968; up until the present revised edition (American Psychiatric Association, 1994) each ensuing *DSM* volume has given more explicit criteria for recognising personality disorders. The criteria are clusters of behavioural, emotional and cognitive patterns marking a particular personality style.

It is important to note that diagnostic systems such as the *DSM* are often criticised because they are based on clinical judgements, agreed by committees of experienced psychiatrists, rather than on empirical evidence from large-scale research. The systems, which are heavily weighted with descriptions of symptoms, also lack any underlying theory with explanatory power (Stevens and Price, 1996). They are thus open to a 'reifying' tendency which, because of the weight of descriptive detail, may result in a phenomenon like 'social phobia' being accepted as more discrete and concrete than it actually is. Whilst we agree with these criticisms, and do not necessarily accept the labels as completely true, we still find the systems useful. Their descriptions of behavioural, emotional, physiological and cognitive factors which may be found together can help the therapist to identify the general ground she is working on.

The following illustrate three types of personality disorders likely to be found amongst a cognitive therapist's caseload: those of the dependent, avoidant and borderline personalities. The characteristics are taken from the *Diagnostic and Statistical Manual*; the World Health Organisation has a similar manual called the *International Classification of Diseases*, 10th Edition, or *ICD-10* (WHO, 1993), containing similar criteria for personality disorders.

DSM-IV – Criteria for Dependent Personality Disorder
A pervasive and excessive need to be taken care of that leads to submissive and clinging behavior and fears of separation, beginning by early adulthood and present in a variety of contexts, as indicated by five (or more) of the following:

1. has difficulty making everyday decisions without an excessive amount of advice and reassurance from others
2. needs others to assume responsibility for most major areas of his or her life
3. has difficulty expressing disagreement with others because of fear of loss of support or approval. **Note:** Do not include realistic fears of retribution.
4. has difficulty initiating projects or doing things on his or her own (because of a lack of self-confidence in judgement or abilities rather than a lack of motivation or energy)
5. goes to excessive lengths to obtain nurturance and support from others, to the point of volunteering to do things that are unpleasant
6. feels uncomfortable or helpless when alone because of exaggerated fears of being unable to care for himself or herself

7. urgently seeks another relationship as a source of care and support when a close relationship ends
8. is unrealistically preoccupied with fears of being left to take care of himself or herself.
        (American Psychiatric Association, 1994, p. 284)

DSM-IV – Criteria for Avoidant Personality Disorder
A pervasive pattern of social inhibition, feelings of inadequacy, and hypersensitivity to negative evaluation, beginning by early adulthood and present in a variety of contexts, as indicated by four (or more) of the following:

1. avoids occupational activities that involve significant interpersonal contact, because of fears of criticism, disapproval or rejection
2. is unwilling to get involved with people unless certain of being liked
3. shows restraint within intimate relationships because of the fear of being shamed or ridiculed
4. is preoccupied with being criticised or rejected in social situations
5. is inhibited in new interpersonal situations because of feelings of inadequacy
6. views self as socially inept, personally unappealing or inferior to others
7. is unusually reluctant to take personal risks in any new activities because they may prove embarrassing.
        (American Psychiatric Association, 1994, p. 283)

DSM-IV – Criteria for Borderline Personality Disorder
A pervasive pattern of instability of interpersonal relationships, self-image, and affects, and marked impulsivity beginning by early adulthood and present in a variety of contexts, as indicated by five (or more) of the following:

1. frantic efforts to avoid real or imagined abandonment. **Note:** Do not include suicidal or self-mutilating behavior covered in Criterion 5.
2. a pattern of unstable and intense interpersonal relationships characterised by alternating extremes of idealisation and devaluation
3. identity disturbance: marked and persistently unstable self-image or sense of self
4. impulsivity in at least two areas that are potentially self-damaging (e.g., spending, sex, substance abuse, reckless driving, binge eating). **Note:** Do not include suicidal or self-mutilating behavior covered in Criterion 5.
5. recurrent suicidal behavior, gestures, or threats, or self-mutilating behavior
6. affective instability due to a marked reactivity of mood (e.g., intense episodic dysphoria, irritability or anxiety usually lasting a few hours and only rarely more than a few days
7. chronic feelings of emptiness

8. inappropriate intense anger or difficulty controlling anger (e.g., frequent displays of temper, constant anger, recurrent physical fights)
9. transient, stress-related paranoid ideation or severe dissociative symptoms.

(American Psychiatric Association, 1994, pp. 280-1)

Personality Disorder: Mad and Beyond Help

Our initial reaction to the term 'personality disorder' (PD) was the image of 'craziness' in the mould of a Gothic novel. Something, in other words, rare, sick, dangerous and probably very difficult to work with. A review of each of these descriptions in turn will take us far in our attempt to come to terms with the concept.

Rare

Attempts to assess the exact prevalence of PDs according to the types of criteria specified in *DSM* and *ICD* classifications are made difficult by the relatively poor degree to which even expert therapists can agree on their presence in particular clients. This is further aggravated by the fact that the disorders themselves are considered to be frequently present in multiple form. De Girolamo and Reich review international evidence on the prevalence of PDs across many cultures and conclude:

Firstly, as shown by most recent epidemiological surveys, PDs are common and have been found in different countries and socio-cultural settings; secondly, PDs can be very detrimental to the life of the affected individual and highly disruptive to societies, communities and families . . . ' (1993, p. 1)

It is also important to remember that the surveys have been conducted using, by and large, *DSM* and *ICD-10* criteria and that, it is our belief that many people, including counsellors and therapists, show significant PD clustering at sub-*DSM* level. When we have shown the criteria to other counsellors and therapists, they have been only too able to recognise particular personality problem areas in themselves. This, in our view, has the ironical possibility that, whilst labels are often viewed as oppressive, identification of particular labels in ourselves might lead to a liberating and democratising influence. It may well be that we are all on a continuum of personality disorders, thereby helping the therapist to take a 'normalising' attitude when dealing with clients with significant PD clusters.

Sick

The stereotyping tag of sickness, major breakdown and/or psychotic behaviour is inaccurate because, by definition, PDs are specifically non-psychotic. The personality disorder most suggestive of mental illness, 'Schizoid Personality Disorder', excludes schizophrenia. Personality disorders do not preclude 'good' or 'normal' social functioning and may even enhance certain types of role functioning. For example, a dependent personality may be very well suited to life in the lower ranks of the military. Some have also suggested that an obsessive-compulsive personality might make a good librarian or cognitive therapist. Whilst it could be argued that such personality traits would be unlikely to lead to any real sense of happiness and fulfilment in the long run, clients with personality disorders can function quite well over long periods. Problems may only arise when the dysfunctional beliefs and schemata underlying the PD become triggered or exposed by events – for example, when a client with strong dependent features, believing 'I need someone close at hand at all times', loses the person designated to hold that role for them.

Dangerous

The view of the personality-disordered client as dangerous, running amok and causing random damage and injury probably only relates to one specific personality disorder – Antisocial Personality Disorder. Antisocial Personality Disorder has the smallest prevalence for any PD. However, as a result of their occasional or potential antisocial actions, these people are likely to attract attention to themselves, and are more dangerous than average clients, holding beliefs such as 'People will get me if I don't get them first' (Beck et al., 1990). However, such 'antisocial' personalities do not usually act in an uncontrolled way: in fact, planning is a feature of their behaviour. The real question, though, is whether the identification of the label of Antisocial Personality Disorder helps the therapist. Whilst there may be some danger of a 'self-fulfilling prophecy', there is also the countervailing benefit that early recognition could help the therapist to be more understanding of the client and thus more able to make more accurate predictions about the client, thereby helping him or her to be less dangerous.

Impossible to Treat

The perception that PDs are impossible to work with is held fairly widely within the helping professions. It may well have operated as a negative label which has denied these people access to treatment services. This situation is now hopefully beginning to change, alongside the significant growth of interest in this field in recent years, across different therapeutic schools (Abend et al., 1983; Beck et al., 1990; Layden et al., 1993; Linehan, 1987). No therapists working with PD issues would argue that the work is easy, but they would want to change the word 'impossible' to 'difficult but possible'. Beck et al., review the as yet small number of studies assessing the efficacy of cognitive-behavioural approaches to PDs and note that in certain areas such as avoidance, the evidence is that 'many clients with personality disorders can be treated quite effectively' (1990, p. 21).

Schema Issues – A More Constructive Approach

At the end of this plea for counsellors to look for what might be useful in the concept of 'personality disorder', we are still unhappy with the actual term itself. If it is consistently misunderstood and stereotyped amongst professionals, the term is likely to be similarly perceived amongst clients. It is therefore not a term that we would consider using with clients. Fortunately, a more user-friendly term and concept is emerging in cognitively oriented work – schema or schemata (plural).

The schema concept has a considerable history in psychology, for such a young science at least. It was used by Piaget (1952) and Bartlett (1932). The term 'schemata' referred then, as it does in Beck's work, to enduring, deep cognitive structures or 'templates' which are particularly important in structuring perceptions and building up 'rule-giving' behaviours. In Beck's initial work, there was a distinction between surface cognitions – automatic thoughts – and underlying cognitive structures – assumptions and schemata. As cognitive therapy has developed, there has been a growing tendency to distinguish between assumptions and schemata, the latter now being seen as a deeper level of cognition and more likely to be unconditional. For example, the schema 'I'll never be accepted' contrasts with the conditional assumption 'I may be accepted if I work very hard at pleasing people'.

Another way of thinking about the deepest level of cognition is to consider the development of core beliefs. As we descend into the deeper levels of belief, the broader and more 'primitive' cognitions move from the surface thoughts through to core beliefs and schemata, as the following illustrates:

1 *Negative automatic thought*: 'These people don't respect me.' The thought states that the people in this specific situation do not respect me. Despite the discomfort of this specific situation, however, it may be that in many other situations most people do in fact appear to respect me.

2 *Dysfunctional assumption*: 'If I work very hard, even though many people appear not to respect me, it may be possible to get some of them to respect me.'

3 *Core belief*: 'Nobody really respects me.' No matter what I do, however hard I try to please people by working hard, no matter how much I search, I can't seem to find any people who respect me.

4 *Early maladaptive schema*: A 'felt sense' of 'shame' in relationships, that one counts for little or nothing. A consistent perception of indifference or violation from close significant others, most likely from parents, resulting in a profound sense of worthlessness which colours most situations one finds oneself in.

Core beliefs are therefore the central foundation of self-concept. Some writers use the terms 'schema' and 'core belief' interchangeably, but Beck (1964) distinguishes between schemata as cognitive structures, such as an 'unworthiness' schema, and core beliefs as specific content of the schemata, such as 'I am unworthy', 'I don't measure up', or 'Others are better than me'.

Jeffrey Young's Early Maladaptive Schema (EMS) and 'Lifetraps'

Young was an early associate of Beck's and the director of training at the Cognitive Therapy Center in Philadelphia in the early 1980s. Towards the end of the 1980s, he began to develop a form of cognitive therapy that was suitable for clients with personality disorders (Young, 1994). The work evolved as he began to realise that clients with personality issues did not always respond to standard cognitive therapy. For example, a feature of Avoidant Personality Disorder would be the lack of close confiding relationships which would influence the therapeutic relationship, such as in the client not trusting the therapist's feedback (Beck et al., 1990). Another example would be the over-compliant aspect of dependent personality behaviour, which could influence the client to give the therapist 'welcome news' of favourable evidence rather than developing what the therapy requires – the ability to identify, sift and present evidence of all kind. In his 1994 publication, Young was aware of the difficulties surrounding the label of personality disorder and began to develop the 'schema-focused approach'. Rather than use the labels provided by the *DSM* classifications, he identified 18 Early Maladaptive Schema (EMS) patterns in five general domains – Disconnection and Rejection; Autonomy and Performance; Impaired Limits; Other-Directedness; Overvigilance and Inhibition. These schema patterns might operate multiply. The book carries an addendum with a self-rated inventory to help one identify which schema issues might be active in a client's or one's own life. Each domain has a number of schemata within it – for example, Abandonment/Instability and Mistrust/Abuse are schemata within the Disconnection and Rejection domain. The characteristics of schemata are shown in Figure 6.1

A schema is a relatively enduring, deep cognitive structure that organises the principles of giving appraisal and meaning to experiences, especially in relation to rules of living, with regard to self, others and the world.

Schemata are:

- unconditional;
- usually not immediately available to consciousness;
- latent and can be active or dormant according to the presence or absence of triggering events;
- neither 'good' nor 'bad' but may be considered functional or dysfunctional in how well they fit the client's actual life experiences, and cherished life goals;
- compelling or non-compelling to the extent in which they are active and influential in the client's life;
- pervasive or narrow in the extent to which they influence the client's life, especially the number of areas in which they are active.

Figure 6.1   *The characteristics of schemata*

Young and Klosko (1993) note that

> schemas are central to our sense of *self*. To give up our belief in a schema would be to surrender the security of knowing who we are and what the world is like; therefore we cling to it, even when it hurts us. These early beliefs provide us with a sense of predictability and certainty; they are comfortable and familiar. In an odd sense, they make us feel at home. (1993, p. 6)

In *Reinventing Your Life*, designed as a self-help book for clients, Young and Klosko (1993) use the perhaps more friendly term 'lifetraps' to describe schemata. The book also contains a simplified questionnaire to help clients identify which of the 11 specified lifetraps may play a role in their difficulties. It seems that Young changed the number of schematic patterns for a popularised version of his concepts rather than for theoretical reasons. It is not yet clear whether these concepts will be further developed and researched. In any case, they do represent one of the first attempts to spell out in more detail how the evolving schema-focused model might actually work in practice.

Young also clearly spells out the concept of schema maintenance. Early Maladaptive Schemata may be particularly rigid and resistant to change. This resistance will be reinforced by particular behaviours, thoughts and beliefs. For example, a client with a mistrust schema may well create almost impossible conditions of trust for others to comply with. The other person's inevitable lack of compliance with these impossible conditions will then of course reconfirm the client's original belief that other people simply cannot be trusted. Padesky (1993b) makes the helpful metaphor of a maladaptive schema as a prejudice template, a prejudice not easily being open to evidence which contradicts its assumptions. This can be a useful analogy for clients who are unfailingly guided by their maladaptive schemata. The metaphor will be posed in the form of a question such as: 'How much faith could a woman looking for personal advice have in a misogynistic adviser?'

The Development of Schemata

Bowlby (1985) writes how Beck's model of psychopathology was compatible with his own more psychodynamic model, yet also noted that Beck did not offer any full explanation of how schemata develop from early experience. This criticism has been taken up by cognitive therapists such as Beck himself (Beck et al., 1990), Jeffrey Young (Young, 1994; Young and Klosko, 1993) and Mary Ann Layden (Layden et al., 1993). Layden et al. (1993) have opened up new ground in cognitive therapy by drawing links between cognitive formulations and developmental concepts such as those of Erikson (1963) and Piaget (1952). The development of schemata comes from the particular way in which life events are evaluated and translated into ways of seeing self, others and the world at particular stages of development. Difficult or traumatic early experience is likely to be particularly influential, depending on the developmental stages the child is going through. For example, very early experiences, between 0 and 2 years of age, can be conceptualised against Erikson's psycho-sexual stage of 'trust versus mistrust'. A bad experience of an untrustworthy care-giving adult during this period would strongly relate to the development of a 'mistrust schema'. Without some kind of resolution, this could result in long-term difficulties in trusting others. A mistrust schema, as has been referred to several times in this book, is a frequently met client interpersonal difficulty. It is highly likely that this schema will be replayed within therapy itself.

Mary Ann Layden has given cognitive therapy the valuable concept of 'The Cloud'. When children are very young, being either pre-verbal or with only very limited verbal development, they cannot encode and store experience in ways that they will be able to later on in life, lacking sophisticated verbal processing and memory retention. Piaget (1952) describes early child thinking styles as 'pre-operational' (that is, lacking the logical operations characteristic of later stages) and 'magical' (that is, wrong, usually over-personalised, causal thinking), and these might lead to 'black and white' (reducing several categories to just two) thinking and 'personalisation' (seeing oneself as more personally implicated than one is) in relation to the schema. However, recent neonate and infant research shows that very young children are extremely sensitive to visual, auditory and kinaesthetic cues in the environment. These then form the hazy mélange of experience which Layden calls 'The Cloud'. Where there have been very powerful early maladaptive experiences such as abuse, neglect or inconsistency, the child learns that the world is not a good place and that others cannot be trusted. Since they are not able to understand the motives of care-givers, they may conclude that the only explanation for their predicament must lie in their own 'badness'.

By the time the client reaches therapy as an adult, such trauma is likely to be a relatively inaccessible mélange of 'bad' visceral feeling with very fragmented accompanying cognitions. Because of the visceral haziness of the 'The Cloud', the child, and later the adult, has few retrieval clues to access the memories, which means that they cannot be well processed, cognitively or emotionally. Like the 'fear structure' of Foa and Kozak (1986), the experiences may lie like an unmeltable block of ice close to the surface of the mind. They can be easily triggered as overwhelming emotion at any time. As the memories themselves are not easily retrievable, the experience of overwhelming emotion may be all the more baffling and scary to the client herself and to those around her.

> Lorna had strong schematic memories from childhood. In these memories, she was accused by her parents of having failed to discharge duties that most people would consider unfair impositions on a young child, such as being able to anticipate that her younger brother might fall in a pond whilst she was responsible for him. She did not then have the sophisticated conceptual thinking that would have been necessary to defend herself. This schema is now activated when she is unfairly criticised at work. The discharge of feeling which results from the activation of the schema prevents her from being able to find any of her normal adult responses, so that, as in childhood, powerlessness and humiliation are experienced.

The integration of schemata into the cognitive model has had an important influence on the development and practice of cognitive therapy. For example, when a therapist is aiming to help the adult client develop more flexible and functionally adaptable ways of thinking, he may be dealing with pre-verbal experience, resulting in severe limitations in using a highly verbal intervention to try to impact on these schemata.

The Past – An Area Where the Cognitive Therapist Need Not Fear to Tread

Cognitive therapy initially inherited the behaviourist's unwillingness to attribute very much significance to childhood experience. In 1970, Beck contrasted cognitive therapy and psychoanalytic therapy on several counts, including the observation that 'neither cognitive nor behavior therapy draws substantially on recollections or reconstruction of the patient's childhood experiences and early family relationships. The emphasis on correlating present problems with developmental events, furthermore, is much less prominent than in psychoanalytic psychotherapy' (Beck, 1970b, p. 185). It may be that there is some truth in the accusation that cognitive therapy as initially formulated was heavy on pragmatics and somewhat light on theory. As the therapy has developed, and as it has encountered more clients who could not be helped by the original parsimonious version, it may have been inevitable that there has been more interest in the causation of psychopathology. There has been a noticeable increase in thinking on historical causation from both Beck and others, especially since Bowlby noted that cognitive therapy had no real explanation of how schemata developed (Holmes, 1993). That cognitive schemata were related to early experience was fully acknowledged by Beck right from the very start: 'These assumptions . . . may be derived from childhood experiences, or from attitudes and opinions of peers or parents' (Beck et al., 1979, p. 245). The early emphasis on short-term work may have limited the imaginative scope of cognitive therapists in devising ways of working in this area.

In 1980, Lazarus predicted that as cognitive therapy developed, it would tend towards 'psychodynamic therapy revisited', and Power (1991) detected a 'psychoanalytic drift' in cognitive therapy. Schema work is now a developing field and new and imaginative ways, some close to psychodynamic methods, are being used – for example by Mary Ann Layden and her colleagues. They have been very interested in the concept of 'countertransference', particularly in relation to clients with personality disorders. Borderline clients often seem to show a kind of 'push–pull' in relationships. They desperately want intimacy but are very afraid of it so that they are likely to encourage a relationship but then move sharply away as the other person gets close. They are very likely to exercise this kind of 'interpersonal pull' (Safran and Segal, 1990) on the therapist, who is likely to get frustrated, as other people in their lives do. As well as the ability to 'work through' these types of crises in the therapeutic relationship, as would be done in other therapies, the schema-focused cognitive therapist also has the understanding of schemata and core beliefs which could be operating here. In the above example, the client might have two contradictory core beliefs: 'I must get close because without a partner, I'm nothing' and 'Opening myself to others means I'm very vulnerable'. Rather like the 'fear network' of Foa and Kozak (1986), the client may have something like an 'interpersonal fear network' in which all these beliefs and assumptions become activated at once in an overwhelming mélange of negative emotions.

Working with Schemata

Working at the level of Symptoms versus Schemata
One of the ways that early models of cognitive therapy distinguished themselves from psychodynamic therapy was the firm position they adopted regarding the desirability of starting with present experience, in particular, working at the symptom level. Cognitive therapy, as we have discussed before, works from the principle of parsimony – beginning with work at the symptom level, especially with automatic thoughts. For example, Beck et al. (1979) stressed that when people are very depressed, they often feel hopeless and find it difficult to concentrate. Both of these factors limit the client's capacity to enter into 'insight' work. Trying to 'work through' the depressive symptoms by experiential techniques alone may not only prove inadequate but may even worsen the level of bad feelings. Such work becomes more possible as some of the symptoms of depression begin to lift. Cognitive therapy of depression therefore often *starts* with work at the behavioural level, aiming for at least some lessening of bad feeling. Blackburn and Davidson (1995) estimate that around 75 per cent of the intervention in standard cognitive therapy of depression is concerned with symptom-level work, typically working with behavioural responses to the passivity of depression and the countering of negative automatic thoughts experienced by the depressed person. The remaining quarter of treatment may be concerned with underlying issues and preventative strategies.

As the work proceeds and the counsellor builds up a conceptualisation, deeper beliefs, including core beliefs, become evident. It may of course be that in working directly on behavioural passivity and hopelessness, one is already working on underlying schemata such as 'I am cursed' or 'I cannot act powerfully in my life'. As this present-oriented and symptom-level work unfolds, most clients will begin to reveal certain facts about previous experiences, including childhood experiences. The cognitive therapist is able to use the conceptualisation to fit all these pieces of information into the overall picture. The therapist may, for example, invite the client to talk about childhood experiences and then ask, 'What beliefs or rules of living do you think developed from those experiences?' It is often surprising that clients can quite easily describe clear, often stark, core beliefs that they were not previously consciously aware of. However, schemata are unlikely to become a major focus of therapy unless the client actually puts them on the agenda or the therapist begins to conclude that such underlying issues are likely to predispose the client to a relapse of symptoms unless tackled therapeutically.

We have found that where the client's pre-morbid functioning was reasonably good, without marked personality disturbance, it may often be enough to merely unveil the core beliefs, alerting the client to them and raising awareness of how they operate – particularly the way they are triggered and how they send disturbed feeling 'cascading' down to the symptom level. It may not always be necessary to work on modifying the core beliefs – the client's increased awareness of the beliefs in itself leads to changes, as the following illustrates.

Keith, a 40-year-old computer project worker, had been prone to depression and anxiety since adolescence. He became depressed again after his job became threatened by organisational changes at work. He had frequent negative automatic thoughts such as, 'I'm falling behind at work', 'They think my work is under par', 'They thought my report was rubbish', and 'The others are way ahead of me'. The counselling was limited to a maximum of eight sessions. In the first six sessions, Keith was able to learn cognitive techniques and, in particular, to vigorously challenge his negative automatic thoughts. His BDI score fell from 23 to 8 (from moderate depression to non-problematic functioning). During these early sessions, Keith occasionally spoke about his childhood, usually rather reluctantly. His description was of an 'unremarkable' childhood and it seemed difficult to link this with his 'worrying' cognitive style. In session 6, the client and I (FW) went over this again and tried to draw out a formulation together. Keith suddenly said, 'The thing is they didn't seem to worry about me . . . maybe they didn't worry enough.' I (FW) added, 'Did that leave you to do all the worrying?' In session 7, Keith reported that this question had led to an 'Ah-ha' experience and he surprised me by bringing in a very detailed formulation he had worked on by himself, with two pages of closely written textual notes with examples of his childhood experiences. This was talked through in session 7 and as part of his 'blueprint' at the end of therapy (see Chapter 8), but was not otherwise 'worked through'. Keith reported himself happy to finish therapy at the end of session 8. His feedback included positive comments of how helpful it had been to look at some of the historical roots of his difficulties.

Schema-Focused Therapy as the Main Intervention

The 'standard' (that is, short-term) model of cognitive therapy often proceeds as we have described above: moving from symptoms to assumptions to the identification of schemata and possibly some work at that level. If there are clear indications that the client's history is playing a dominant role in the evolution of his difficulties, and where standard cognitive therapy needs to be adapted to the client's particular issues, then we would begin to think in terms of 'schema-focused' cognitive therapy. Schema-focused work is likely to result in a longer-term version of the therapeutic intervention. Such clear indications might include the following:

1 Clear trauma emerging from early and/or previous experience.
2 Deeper 'themes' emerging strongly in the client's material.
3 Apparent failure of early attempts to achieve some symptom relief.
4 The client requests longer-term therapy focused on early experience.

At the two ends of the continuum between work focused mainly on 'here and now' symptomatology and that focused on 'there and then' underlying issues, there is a grey area of middle ground where these decisions about the foci and length of therapy are perhaps more difficult. For the moment, we will talk about the underlying issues mode but will return to the grey area towards the end of this chapter.

Schema-Focused Cognitive Therapy as Homeopathic Healing

One interesting, though often overlooked, aspect of therapy is the extent to which different models of therapy emphasise and/or mix allopathic and homeopathic principles. The allopathic principle opposes a pathogenic phenomenon with an equally strong or stronger anti-pathogenic force. In terms of schema-focused therapy, the schema is attacked until it is fatally undermined or at least helpfully modified. The homeopathic principle is that the pathogenic phenomenon is stimulated by a further controlled dose of the pathogenic force itself and so, after an initial worsening, the pathogenic force runs its course and thereby stimulates natural healing forces. In schema-focused therapy terms, this may mean 'staying with' the schema, experiencing it and its contradictions fully before making any change and so letting the change unfold.

The allopathic perspective is strongly represented in the traditional model of cognitive therapy, with its emphasis on short-term active therapeutic effort oriented towards change. The homeopathic perspective is strongly represented in psychodynamic, especially Jungian therapy. Moore (1992), for example, argues that the saturnine aspects of depression are not something to be seen as entirely negative. They contain the seeds of acceptance of the darker side of life, especially death, and can be symbolic of ageing and the development of wisdom. Beck (1987) and other cognitively oriented writers such as Gilbert (1984, 1989, 1992a, 1992b) have written of the evolutionary functions of depression, characterised by the conservation of energy following deprivation or defeat. The confluence of different therapeutic concepts is seen in a growing number of books on therapy, healing and evolution (such as Nesse and Williams, 1995; Stevens and Price, 1996). It seems that 'melancholy', a once fashionable pose for Elizabethan poets, becomes depression when this functional, even comforting, sadness goes into a negative cycle which prevents normal resumption of activity following a period of withdrawal. The recovery reaction, however, will be highly individually mediated according to the person's world-view and general social environment. There may be times when it is helpful for the client to get more in touch with their sense of sadness, sounding its ocean floor to see if there is anything of value there. It may be that successful cognitively based therapeutic work is only possible when enough of this often denied feeling is activated. Equally, it may be that there are times when the sad feeling needs to be moved on.

The concepts of 'emotional processing' developed by Foa and Kozak (1986) in relation to anxiety may be matched by an analogous situation in depression. In working with fear, enough of the fear needs to be raised for processing to begin, without over-activating the 'fear structure' and leading to the 'shutting down' of emotional and/or cognitive reprocessing. In depression, therefore, processing may occur when the depression is active, again without overloading the individual with depression so that processing is impossible. We believe that the issue of emotional processing is somewhat under-discussed in current cognitive approaches, which may lead the reader to conclude that the cognitive therapist would always work against depression in an allopathic way. The cognitive therapy literature seems to have had little to say about the circumstances when one might stay with a depressed feeling for possible homeopathic benefit. Likewise, other therapies seem curiously inactive in relation to depression, tending to see it as nearly always a sign of an underlying issue. The search for this underlying issue then becomes the main therapeutic strategy. Sometimes, in our opinion, unfruitful arguments between the therapies stem from the fact that allopathic therapy is being compared to unlike homeopathic therapy, or vice versa. In fact, we believe that all therapy contains both allopathic and homeopathic elements and that the newer model of cognitive therapy offers the chance of a particularly felicitous balance of these two elements.

Tools and Techniques for Working with Schemata
Schema-focused cognitive therapy is very much in its infancy and a completely clear model has yet to be articulated. Ways of working with schemata are gradually being developed, particularly through the work of Beck, Padesky, Young and Layden. As we have described above, schema networks may be difficult to access through language alone. Imagery techniques therefore have much to offer in opening them up (Beck et al., 1990; J. Beck, 1995; Edwards, 1989, 1990; Layden et al., 1993; Padesky and Greenberger, 1995; Wells and Hackmann, 1993). The client can be asked to report significant images occurring at moments of difficulty. She may be asked to induce an image of her difficulties or situation, which can then be explored for their incipient meanings. Therapist and client may attempt to transform the meaning and experience of the imagery in ways that may prove more helpful to the client. More language-based interventions can also be used in the form of continua and positive data logs (Padesky, 1994; Padesky and Greenberger, 1995). In continua work the client is asked to map out how he sees himself in relation to others. For example, for the rigid belief 'I'm useless', the therapist would encourage the client to begin to define 'useless' more closely and begin to map out how different people the client knows would make out on the positive and negative criteria evolved. The idea, as in standard cognitive therapy, is to try to 'stretch out' these inflexible categories, so that the client can begin to realise how inaccurate and counterproductive they really are. Positive data logs encourage the client to keep a diary of all the positive self-attributes and achievements he can detect. Positive diaries provide powerful evidence to disconfirm the self-prejudice induced

by maladaptive schemata. (Padesky, 1994, and Padesky and Greenberger, 1995, give a more detailed description of these techniques.)

Responding to Schema Issues in the Therapeutic Relationship
We would like to end this chapter by giving our view of the base-line responses that counsellors have to be prepared to make when they become aware that their client has a schema-based issue. The first thing is obviously to be aware of the schema. This often comes about because the therapist experiences the counter-tranferential 'pull' of the schema. We have drawn up a brief résumé in Figure 6. 2. Fittingly, it owes much to the work of Kahn

---

Phase I – Dealing with one's own countertransference reaction

1 **Do not retaliate**
   Schematic material can be very provoking and disheartening to the therapist. Remember that this is why the person needs therapy. It is just something that they do, not all of what they are that is the problem. Try to 'hold' the difficulty.

2 **Do not offer immediate 'easy' reassurance**
   Being a nice person, you will be very tempted to reassure the client: 'Of course, you can trust me . . .', '. . . I won't abandon you . . .'. If you do this, however, you run the danger of not seizing the moment and taking the chance to work with the schema whilst it is 'hot'. You may also be reacting like other people in the client's life – most usually in a schema-confirming way. Again, try to hold the difficulty and then open it for examination and 'working through'.

Phase II – Responding therapeutically

3 **Express empathy for the schema**
   'It's understandable that, given your circumstance, you've come to think that you can't trust people [i.e. in the case of a mistrust schema]. Most people who'd had those experiences would end up feeling that way.'

4 **Acknowledge the schema and suggest it is a problem that can be solved collaboratively**
   'In a way, it is good that it has come up now. It means that we can take the time to work out ways of stopping it from getting in the way of the things you want to do in your life.'

Figure 6.2   *Responding to schema-triggered reactions that disrupt the therapy process*

(1991), who writes to show how humanistic therapy and psycho-dynamic therapy are converging in their view of the therapeutic relationship. We would like the cognitive voice to be added to this debate.

Conclusion

It is important to acknowledge that there may well be a large 'grey area' concerning the presence of 'schemata' and/or 'personality disorders' in clients and in people, therapists included, in general. Researchers have found it difficult to show that *DSM*-type criteria for 'personality disorders' are consistent across different assessors (De Girolamo and Reich, 1993). Whilst some cognitive therapists have tried to make hard and fast divisions between 'standard' and 'schema-focused' cognitive therapy, we think it is far more likely that the difference will be distributed on a continuum. The significance of this view is that the cognitive therapist may well find herself working on the schema level in both medium- and short-term work as well as in longer-term work. The fact that the cognitive therapist is now much better equipped to work flexibly is one of the most exciting developments of cognitive therapy today.

7

Difficulties in Cognitive Therapy

When reading or hearing about cognitive therapy, it is sometimes possible to gain the impression that cognitive approaches allow for easy case conceptualisation, progressing smoothly into the use of aptly chosen techniques to which the client responds in a positive way, taking on board the model and always doing homework. The result is clear symptom reduction and a happier client. However, things do not always happen like they say in the books. Beck et al. aptly remind us, 'The course of therapy, like true love, is not always smooth' (1979, p. 295). In our experience, the textbook case of cognitive therapy, whilst common enough to allow for a great deal of job satisfaction, is the exception rather than the rule. Not all therapy sessions present major obstacles to be overcome; however, the cognitive therapist has to be on the lookout for difficulties which may arise, sometimes perniciously. Such obstacles may be seen as upsetting the flow of the therapy. They may arise from misunderstandings or the therapist having an 'off day'. Obstacles almost always, if viewed and used in the service of therapy, provide valuable material for both understanding and working with the client. They can facilitate the client's conceptualisation, and give greater understanding of the kinds of problems the client is experiencing, as well as areas the therapist needs to work on. To quote Judith Beck:

> Problems of one kind or another arise with nearly every patient in cognitive therapy . . . [A] reasonable goal is therefore not to avoid problems altogether but rather to learn to uncover and specify problems, to conceptualize how they arose, and to plan how to remediate them. (1995, p. 300)

She also reminds us,

> The therapist who encounters a problem in therapy has a choice. He can catastrophize about the problem and/or blame himself or the patient. Alternatively, he can turn the problem into an opportunity to refine his skills of conceptualization and treatment planning and to improve his technical expertise and his ability to vary therapy in accordance with the specific needs of each individual patient. (p. 311)

In this chapter, we describe the common difficulties facing the cognitive therapist. Obviously, the list is not exhaustive, but we hope to give a flavour of the way cognitive therapy approaches solves such difficulties. The chapter is divided into two sections: common difficulties in carrying out cognitive therapy; and difficulties in the therapeutic relationship. To a large extent, separating difficulties in the therapeutic relationship from other problems is arbitrary. We may see all problems as arising within the context of the therapeutic relationship and therefore constituting a relationship difficulty. However, cognitive therapy, in keeping with its pragmatic philosophy, suggests moving from the most simple level to the more complex, starting with a bottom-up approach. Thus, one might assume first that a problem is caused by a simple misunderstanding rather than diving in at the level of schema or 'client resistance'. Almost always, the main principles of problem-resolution follow the main principles of cognitive therapy: gain regular feedback to find out what kind of problems exist; conceptualise the problems; work collaboratively towards resolution; and work in the most parsimonious way. It is easy to overlook such principles when bogged down with the intricacies and complexities of therapy. Hence, we stress throughout the chapter the value of feedback and supervision to throw light on our difficulties.

Common Difficulties

When is a Problem a Problem?
Some problems are glaringly obvious: the client does not turn up, ends therapy prematurely, makes a complaint against us, and simply does not find the therapy at all helpful. Others are more specific or subtle such as recurrent difficulties in identifying or challenging thoughts or the client never doing homework, but always having a plausible excuse. Judith Beck (1995) summarises the problems that may occur in cognitive therapy as fitting into several categories: diagnosis, conceptualisation and treatment planning; therapeutic alliance; structure and/or pace of the sessions; socialising the client into the cognitive way of working; dealing with automatic thoughts; accomplishing therapeutic goals; and the client's processing of the session content. She goes on to provide a list of questions the therapist can ask himself

whenever problems arise, such as 'Does the client believe, at least somewhat, that therapy can help?'

Cognitive therapy is an empirical and scientific therapy, and a number of measures, such as the BDI and BAI, as well as regular reviews of the client's mood, allow for assessment of whether or not the client is improving or meeting his therapy goals. One of the great strengths of cognitive therapy in identifying difficulties is in its use of regular feedback, throughout and at the end of both therapy and each therapy session. We aim for the client to be able to give us feedback about what is going on, such as 'I don't follow what you're saying', 'That doesn't make sense' or 'You're not understanding/listening to me'. We may pick up problems indirectly: the client agreeing verbally but looking puzzled. However, the ideal of feedback does not always work. Clients may be hesitant to say they do not understand in case they are thought to be stupid or they may not like to question the therapist as an 'authority figure' because of fear of rejection. The therapist, one way or another, may fear negative feedback and therefore not be open to it in the sessions. Hence, the value of ongoing supervision, both with a supervisor and self-supervision. A great deal can be learned by the therapist allowing time at the end of each session to reflect on or listen to tapes of the session, and giving herself supervision and feedback.

Problems in Identifying and Challenging Thoughts

The bedrock of cognitive therapy lies in identifying specific thoughts, relating these thoughts to emotion and other aspects of the client's being, and learning to see alternative perspectives. However, identifying and challenging thoughts is a common area of difficulty. Some clients report that they do not have, or are not aware of, particular thoughts. The client may find it difficult to separate out thoughts and feelings. It is a common experience for the emotion to precede any conscious thinking, leading to difficulties in picking out thoughts from the mass of cognitions and emotions that accompany strong affect. Clients may not tell us what is really going on, fearing that if they describe their thoughts, strange as they often are, we will think them mad. We think many strange, weird and wonderful thoughts most of the time: how many of us would willingly disclose the content of our babbling brains?

It is sometimes difficult to identify the content of negative, fearful or depressing thoughts since the client may describe to us the answer to the thoughts or a positive way of thinking rather than what was really going on. The client may believe that the aim of therapy is to 'think positive' and will therefore be reluctant to describe negative thoughts. For example, when asking anxious clients to describe what they thought might happen in a feared situation, they may say something along the lines of 'Well, I knew nothing would happen', rather than the scared thought of 'I thought I was going to die'. We may need to actively encourage our clients to express what was really going on, mad, crazy or irrational as it may sound, and discuss any fears clients have about speaking their minds. Clients may report thoughts in the form of questions, such as 'Why me?' when something bad happens to them. It is often useful to seek out their implicit answers to the question to obtain the meaning: for example, 'I'm cursed'. It is very difficult to challenge a thought such as 'Why me?', whereas the concept of the client being cursed, or deserving bad things happening to him, can be explored.

There are various solutions to difficulties in identifying thoughts. Some people relate their important emotions more to images than to words. Therefore, thoughts can be identified by using imagery, asking if the client gets a picture in her mind. It may be helpful to use metaphor: 'Is there something that represents how you felt?', when talking about what the image represents and its meanings (Wells and Hackmann, 1993). Finding the right questions to ask in order to elicit thoughts may involve a process of trial and error: for example, by asking 'Why were you feeling that way?', the therapist might expect the client to say, 'Because I was thinking what a lousy person I am', whereas the 'why' question may elicit: 'I don't know', or 'Because I was feeling bad'. Putting words into the client's mouth is sometimes tempting, but generally best avoided; however, it can be valuable to say something along the lines of 'I guess if it was me, I might be thinking . . . ' or 'A lot of people who feel like that think x; I wonder if that is true for you too?'

IT MAKES SENSE . . . BUT . . .   The 'yes . . . but . . .' syndrome is a common problem, where the client agrees in principle with the idea being discussed yet 'buts' it: 'I understand that I'm thinking very negatively, but I do not know how to change.' Buts are common on thought records: the client may come up with an alternative thought, but then overrules it with a 'yes . . . but . . .'. One answer is to treat the 'but' in the way of any other negative thought, using downward arrow approaches to understand what underlies the word. For example, Sasha, an insurance clerk whom we described in Chapter 1, had a long-standing problem with worry, leading to many physical symptoms and inability to get on with many aspects of her life without paralysing anxiety. She had a great deal of knowledge about ways of managing worry and stress and was able to challenge her worrying thoughts, but it made no difference to how she felt. Every discussion and intervention led to her saying 'I know all that . . . but . . . it doesn't make any difference, or it's too difficult'. Sasha and I (DS) looked at her beliefs about worrying, discussing the role of worry in her life, in particular her constant worrying that she did something wrong at work.

> *Therapist*: What are the disadvantages for you of worrying so much?
> *Sasha*: I know it is making me feel awful. It's so difficult going to work. My husband is getting fed up with me. They must be fed up with me at work asking if I've done it properly. I know all that. I know practically every time I worry about something it turns out OK and I wonder why I made such a fuss. I know I'm being stupid . . .
> *Therapist*: But . . .?
> *Sasha*: But I just can't stop worrying.
> *Therapist*: You know it's 'stupid' but you can't stop it. It's like you know in your head but something else is telling you to worry. How about we hear from the something else . . . the 'but'?
> *Sasha*: But if I didn't worry, I might make a real mess up of my job: I have to worry about it because if I didn't then I might miss something: I'd make a mistake and not even know about it!
> *Therapist*: And then what?
> *Sasha*: I'd just want to die: people would think 'she's made a real mess'.
> *Therapist*: So I guess the but is protecting you from making a mess: like an insurance policy against rejection?
> *Sasha*: Yes, but . . . I guess it is an expensive one.
> *Therapist*: So how about looking at whether you need to be insured in the first place. Or at least find a cheaper policy.
> *Sasha*: Yes, but . . . it's kind of terrifying thinking about being under-insured.

The 'yes . . . but's' had many strands for Sasha, requiring unpacking her fears about change which she found very difficult to articulate. Using downward arrow techniques and metaphors can help to explore the underlying issues, arriving at the emotion rather than challenging thoughts on the surface level. For Sasha, once she recognised her real terror of changing, she began to substitute the word 'and' instead of 'but' whenever she thought to herself about changing. A simple cognitive shift enabled her to acknowledge and recognise her feelings, rather than allowing them to 'but' her into her old patterns of worrying.

CHALLENGING FACTS NOT DISTORTIONS   Sometimes what sounds like a juicy negative thought to challenge is more like a reality, and to try to look for alternatives leaves the client feeling misunderstood, or her difficulties trivialised. For example, Moira was feeling awful as a result of thinking about her relationship with her son: she believed that she had been a bad mother. Moira and I (DS) attempted to look at alternatives to this way of thinking: What was the evidence for her being a bad mother? What was the evidence against? For Moira, the evidence against her being a bad mother was thin on the ground. Her child had been taken into care at a young age because Moira was extremely depressed and unable to cope with her baby; when she was finally reunited with her child, they had not bonded and were unable to form a good relationship. Therefore, it seemed nonsensical for Moira to look at ways in which she had been a good mother. Instead, we talked around the meaning of her not being a good mother: her beliefs that having a child automatically meant that she should have been a good parent; how difficult it had been, because of her circumstances, to look after her baby; how she had done the best for her child by putting him into care. Moira's belief that she was not a good mother did not change; however, she began to be slightly more accepting of her difficulties, and look instead at her feelings of loss for her child.

Stirling Moorey (1996) describes how Beck's model developed in relation to relatively stable emotional states such as clinical depression and anxiety. The model has to be modified to fit situations where a client is adapting to strongly adverse life events. In this case, the emphasis is on the client's distorted way of thinking about the adjustment process itself, as shown in Moira's example. Moorey's research shows that cognitive counselling is more effective than supportive counselling, even in such strongly aversive situations as suffering from severe illness.

'I UNDERSTAND IT IN MY HEAD: BUT I DO NOT FEEL ANY DIFFERENT' Another frequent difficulty is in the process of the working through of therapeutic change. Dryden (1987) describes such working through as going from 'intellectual insight' to 'emotional insight', a process actually evident in most forms of therapy. Therefore, in cognitive therapy, the client may find the therapy makes intellectual sense but not result in feeling any different. Sometimes this can be a matter of repetition and what Ellis (1962) calls 'work and practice': if the client has felt this way for a long time it will take time and practice to change. The time taken to work through from the head level to the gut feelings can be normalised by the therapist and may even be worth anticipating at the early stages of therapy. At other times, the client's difficulties in feeling any different are an indication that one needs to move to another cognitive level. For example the difficulties may be coded not in language but, rather, in other sensory modalities: 'The Cloud' described by Layden et al. (1993).

Therefore the use of language, such as in challenging thoughts, can produce intellectual but not emotional shift. Alternatively, a 'thought' may in fact be an assumption or core belief, suggesting that work needs to move from verbal or behavioural challenging to schema-focused therapy.

Difficulties with Homework

Homework is an integral part of cognitive therapy, and, indeed, completion of homework is linked with the success or otherwise of therapy (Beck et al., 1979; Persons et al., 1988). Homework also presents some of the most common difficulties in cognitive therapy, often simply being forgotten or otherwise not completed, not understood, or itself causing the client problems. Whilst it is gratifying for both client and therapist for homework to proceed smoothly, difficulties with homework can also be a vital part of therapeutic change, allowing for understanding of the problems the client is facing in 'real life' and enabling the client to work them through. The conceptualisation can be very useful in dealing with difficulties with homework. Some clients' responses to homework can be anticipated early on in therapy: for example, clients who are very perfectionistic, or obsessional, may well be paralysed by the need to produce the perfect homework, or be unable to complete a thought record unless every single thought is recorded, a task which becomes so onerous as to be 'best forgotten'. Where, for example, procrastination is part of the client's picture, homework can prove both a useful behavioural experiment and a source of further data.

One obvious problem arises when the therapist does not ask the client, from one week to another, how she got on with homework, thus giving a powerful message that the work was not really necessary or valuable. Therefore, reviewing homework must be integrated into the beginning of every session. Another common problem is that the client simply forgets the homework. It is therefore necessary to have some written record, for both client and therapist, of what the homework was; in addition, we have consistently found therapy tapes to be a valuable reminder for our clients. The client may fear the therapists' response if homework is not done 'correctly', awakening previous experiences of being chastised for things going wrong. It may be that the client does not know how to do the assignment, and both therapist and client were unaware of this. For example, a socially anxious client was unable to do a homework assignment of holding a short conversation with a colleague at work. Rather than being too anxious about the consequences, he simply did not know how to initiate a conversation. In this case, the task highlighted an important area for the client to work on. The client's response to homework must be accepted in an understanding and collaborative way, viewing difficulties as those to be jointly solved rather than a failure on the part of the client. The relevant therapist skill is the ability to set 'no-lose' homework: whatever happens the client finds the experience valuable (Freeman et al., 1990). Whether the homework is done or not, the results can be analysed in cognitive terms and tied to the formulation.

It is useful, also, to normalise the difficulties the client has in making changes between sessions. We all have examples of goals we would really like to attain: a tidier house; getting more exercise; spending less time watching TV; losing weight; or generally moving towards being 'better' people. However, the desire to change is not actually matched by moves towards putting the changes into practice; such changes are more likely to be sabotaged by a variety of mundane and human factors rather than by subconscious forces. Difficulties in doing homework may then be tackled in the same way as tackling getting started on a variety of projects: is the problem lack of motivation, and if so, what does that mean? Is the problem lack of information? Needing more help from others? Needing to get other tasks out of the way before being able to get down to homework? In this way, understanding the difficulties may lead to simple solutions, or may reveal important issues that need to be addressed.

Dealing with Stuck Points

Cognitive therapy is, no doubt, a challenging therapy to work with, for both therapist and client. Although the basics of counselling are required, we as therapists need to be far more active than in other forms of counselling and therapy. As a result, it is not uncommon for the therapist to get over-concerned about the technical aspects of therapy to an extent that is actually paralysing: rather than listening to what the client has to say, we may be thinking about what kind of intervention may be required, whether we are 'doing it right', and whether we should be reading more journals on the client's difficulties before being able to help the client. Although these technical aspects of therapy are extremely important, they are to be used in the service of therapy rather than to the detriment. It is not uncommon for trainee, as well as more experienced, cognitive therapists to throw all the basics out of the window in order to practise cognitive techniques, but in the process somehow get lost. Again, when unsure where to go next, it is tempting to try yet another technique. However, at stuck points or at points where the therapist is not sure where to go next, it is usually far more helpful to go 'back to basics', and stop, listen, reflect and summarise. Throughout, the solution to stuck points is to collaborate with the client to jointly think of a solution. Simply reflecting back to the client: 'It seems as if we are going round in circles and I am not sure what to do next: what do you think?' allows for more collaboration than just trying something out in the hope that it will work.

Thinking time, for both client and therapist, is essential. Cognitive therapy can be very demanding on the therapist's energy, and not therefore conducive to having an 'off day'. However, we have often been surprised at how such apparent off days, when our brains do not want to do good cognitive therapy, have resulted in extremely useful sessions: when we have gone back to basics, listened more, collected more information, summarised and generally used basic counselling skills, sessions have moved on from a stuck phase to useful material or insights for future work. The concept of going back to basics is also useful for trainees, when feeling that they should be more interventionist but unsure of where to go next. The Gestalt concept of the 'fertile void' can be valuable when used in cognitive therapy. The 'fertile void' describes a place where one is seemingly stuck, where old doors have been closed but new ones have not yet opened. Rather than viewing such a place in a negative light, and rushing forward, the void can be a place to stop, take stock, and reflect before deciding where to go next.

Therapy Results in Little Change
We have emphasised throughout the book the empirical nature of cognitive therapy, seeking to measure what is going on, and measure changes in the client's mood or difficulties brought to counselling. Hence, as therapy proceeds, we regularly assess whether or not the therapy is 'working' or whether either a different way of working, or even a different form of therapy, is required (Beck et al., 1979). If short-term standard cognitive therapy is going to be helpful to the client, some form of change is usually evident after a few sessions. It is always encouraging if client and therapist are able to come up with at least a preliminary conceptualisation of the difficulties in the first session or two, leading, if not to improvements in mood, at least to increased hope that things might get better. This is not always the case, however. Although it is important, and therapeutically effective, for the therapist to be 'upbeat' and optimistic about the therapy, it is also important not to raise false hopes, especially in people who have tried different forms of therapy to no avail. Initially only contracting for a few sessions and reviewing after this time to see if the therapy is on course enables us to be both optimistic and realistic. Should the therapy not work, other solutions such as long-term therapy, referral on to another agency or a combination of therapy and medication may well be called for.

We stress the importance of making realistic expectations about what is possible when clients continue to have severe life difficulties. We, or our client, may have expectations that therapy will enable the scores on the BDI to come to the normal, non-depressed range. However, the client may be able to feel better about herself in sessions, but the messages from partner, friends or family and ongoing social and environmental difficulties are likely to hold more impact and require addressing in order to facilitate long-term change.

LOW MOTIVATION TO CHANGE   Whilst we may assume that our clients want to see us, this may not always be the case. Therapy may arise as a result of family pressures, difficulties in a relationship or generally pressure from others; keeping a job, or avoiding a prison sentence, may be contingent on receiving therapy. Not surprisingly, the client may not be too interested in therapy.

Clients who are severely depressed may also have little motivation to attend or engage in counselling, feeling too hopeless to believe that there is any point in trying to change. Whatever the difficulty in motivation, it clearly needs addressing at an early stage. For the client who is not there of his own free will, finding something that he can, personally, get out of therapy may increase motivation: keeping a relationship or staying out of prison may be one goal, but feeling better or meeting important goals in life is often a more powerful incentive. For severely depressed clients, moving slowly towards increasing levels of activity, using activity scheduling, may increase their general motivation; use of antidepressant medication may also lift the client's mood sufficiently to enable her to engage in the process of change.

We cannot underestimate the effects of the individual's situation and environment on her motivation and ability to change. Whilst the client may be willing, the spouse or family may like things as they are, or resent the therapist for meddling in personal affairs. Helping the client to feel better about herself is extremely difficult when her world includes few or no supportive relationships. The consequences of feeling better, being more assertive, less anxious, and so on, need to be carefully assessed in the context of the individual's world. Sometimes, working with the client's partner or family can be very helpful, exploring their attitudes to and concerns about therapy. Working in the therapeutic world, it is sometimes easy for us to forget that the stigma of mental illness and psychotherapies is still alive and well: we may need to convince the client's partner that we are not aiming to brainwash the client or stuff her head full of 'false memories'.

MISMATCHES   Not all clients are suitable for cognitive therapy, or at least some will need a highly modified form of it. Safran and Segal (1990) have devised a scale for calculating suitability and Dryden and Feltham (1994) have suggested quite wide criteria for brief therapy: it is worth reviewing such criteria, discussed in Chapter 4, when assessing why therapy may not be helping. Just as not all clients may be suitable for cognitive therapy, so the same may be true of counsellors. Most of the things that go wrong in cognitive therapy have an echo in both therapist and client, reminding us of the interpersonal nature of therapy. Counsellors are often embarrassed or reluctant to be seen as directive, which can inhibit the ability to structure the session or set homework. This can lead to a sense of vagueness or halfheartedness in the therapist which can be experienced as confusing to the client. Therefore, at this stage, we move to looking at how difficulties in the therapeutic relationship are identified and resolved in cognitive therapy.

Difficulties in the Therapeutic Relationship

Although it may be tempting to view difficulties in the therapeutic relationship as obstacles to be solved before getting on with the real work of therapy, such difficulties reveal important material about the client, and can be used both to understand the client and his mode of relating to others, and to promote therapeutic change. The therapeutic relationship is an arena in which the client, and therapist, may engage in a variety of schema-driven behaviours, and schema maintenance behaviours can be seen in action. Difficulties in the therapeutic relationship can be used as 'diagnostic cues' to identify schemata, particularly those characterising the personality disorders (Beck et al., 1990; Young, 1994). Safran and Segal (1990) take the view that alliance ruptures often occur when the therapeutic relationship activates an important interpersonal schema. Therefore, constructive resolution of a rupture provides an ideal opportunity to conceptualise, explore, challenge and modify that interpersonal schema. The process of being able to identify difficulties and work with them is, in itself, a major therapeutic intervention. It can be actively used in therapy, particularly where clients have not had the experience of resolving difficulties with others, or where people in the client's life do not have the time or patience to work things through. The process of healing the therapeutic relationship also counteracts unhelpful beliefs such as 'It's no use trying to solve my problems', or 'Other people don't care about my problems'.

Difficulties in the therapeutic relationship can be broadly defined as anything to do with the relationship which means that the basics of the relationship are compromised, or vanish altogether. These basics include therapeutic empathy, respect, unconditional positive regard, listening to the client, keeping the boundaries, keeping a structure both within sessions and across therapy as a whole, as well as working collaboratively with the client. Safran and Segal (1990) define therapeutic alliance 'ruptures' as any form of difficulty when the quality of the therapeutic alliance is strained or impaired. A rupture may be on a continuum from a simple misunderstanding during a session, to more chronic problems affecting the whole counselling.

The cornerstone of cognitive therapy is the collaborative relationship. This, however, is not always easy to achieve, and one of the common relationship difficulties is problems with collaboration. Rather than both client and counsellor working together, in an open manner, to resolve the client's difficulties, the counsellor may become 'the expert' and start to offer directive advice; tasks may be set, not negotiated; the client may become 'over-compliant' or 'non-compliant', for example 'agreeing' with the counsellor on homework tasks and then not carrying them out. The counsellor may get the feeling of being a 'bully', 'teacher' or 'political campaigner' in the sessions. The counsellor may lack empathy, or not be able to understand the client, or have extreme negative or positive feelings towards the client, causing difficulties in remaining an objective collaborator. 'Cognitive transference' describes the process where deeply held beliefs about interpersonal relationships or specific helping relationships, and well-ingrained patterns of behaviour, are repeated in the therapeutic relationship and interfere with the collaborative relationship (Beck et al., 1990; Wright and Davis, 1994; Young, 1994). Beck et al. (1990) identify the kinds of schema underlying problems in collaboration, including themes of distrust of the therapist, personal shame, grievances against others, deprecation of self or others, or fear of rejection. In addition, the client may simply not know how to be collaborative, or may fear change.

Difficulties may express themselves as client 'resistance' (Newman, 1994), where the client may not collaborate or co-operate with counselling, or may 'go through the motions' of counselling without being fully engaged. The client may avoid looking at issues of importance previously agreed on, or avoid feeling or expressing any emotion, making the sessions dry and sterile. Alternatively, the client may express high levels of emotion towards the counsellor (Layden et al., 1993). Other difficulties defined by Persons (1989), among others, include lateness, angry outbursts, excessive compliance, passivity or helplessness and unreasonable requests to change the parameters of therapy.

Problems may also arise if the client and counsellor do not share the same conceptualisation of the client's problems, so both are working to different agendas: the counsellor may have arrived at a working conceptualisation of the client's difficulties, and the client may agree in principle with the model but not believe that it applies to him personally. These differences can cause relationship difficulties even before counselling commences. The therapist may have difficulty in empathising with the client: this may be because of the therapist's assumptions, or what is going on in the client. Problems may arise from the way the therapist is carrying out cognitive therapy: for example, not sharing the conceptualisation; doing the work for rather than with the client; seeing the person as a mass of problems rather than as the person he is; arguing with the client; being overwhelmed by our own feelings; and becoming 'contaminated' by the client, and 'colluding' with his problems. Both client and therapist may end up in the role of client.

Working with Difficulties in the Therapeutic Relationship
Although, on paper, it is possible to define and describe difficulties in the therapeutic relationship, in practice, actual difficulties can be hard to observe and may be missed. The therapeutic relationship involves engagement at the level of emotion and of interpersonal communication which may be non-verbal, and is therefore hard at times to describe. However, when difficulties are encountered, something almost intangible occurs: a vague feeling of discomfort, or behaviours that on the surface look straightforward but do not 'ring true', such as counsellor or client being persistently late for sessions, always armed with a 'good excuse'. A helpful marker is the shift from the sessions seeming 'alive', with a sense of therapist and client working together in an active way, to a 'dead' feeling, where therapist and/or client may be 'going through the motions' of, say, challenging a thought or guided discovery, but without any movement. This may be because the client has cut off from affect, or is finding it difficult to communicate affect to the therapist. Only when stepping back and trying to describe and analyse what is occurring can the difficulties be understood and conceptualised.

Conceptualising Difficulties in the Therapeutic Relationship
One way of conceptualising the therapeutic relationship in order to understand and work with difficulties is to see it as an interaction between three players: the impact of the client, the therapist and the environment, as illustrated in Figure 7.1.

The therapeutic relationship is an arena in which client and therapist operate according to their schemata and assumptions. Whilst the client is the focus of therapy, the role of the therapist

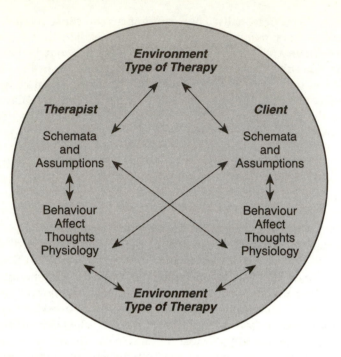

Figure 7.1   *The therapeutic relationship*

should not be neglected, and understanding the conceptualisation of both the client and the therapist is necessary to identify and resolve difficulties in the therapeutic relationship. In addition, these difficulties give us greater information and insight about our client's and our own assumptions and schemata, providing a 'window' on to the client's beliefs, behaviours and expectations as well as our own particular psychology. The third factor is the impact of the environment in which the therapy is conducted. Various factors external to the client and counsellor may cause difficulties in the therapeutic relationship (Wright and Davis, 1994). These include: the type or length of counselling; the situation, such as hospital- versus primary care-based counselling; pressures to 'cure' people in a fixed length of time; social or cultural factors; financial issues; or effects of the client's real life social circumstances. Working in the National Health Service, for example, means that the number of sessions per client is limited, whereas the number of sessions per week for therapists is maximised, both determined by 'the management' as opposed to the client's or therapist's needs. After seeing too many people in a day, we have very little ability to relate to anything other than a television. Difficulties in the therapeutic relationship may reflect a mis-match between the client's needs and the counsellor's style or mode of counselling (Wright and Davis, 1994). For example, the high level of structure, Socratic questioning or empirical approach in cognitive therapy may not suit some clients, being so incompatible with their beliefs and assumptions as to make developing a therapeutic relationship extremely difficult. Whilst some clients may want us to be active and directive, others prefer a non-directive or relatively inactive therapeutic style. Alternatively a less structured form of counselling, focusing on the therapeutic relationship, may be very threatening and difficult for some clients. The client's problems themselves may impinge on the therapeutic relationship: for example, if the client is very depressed and hopeless, the therapist needs to be more energetic and hopeful; panic or phobic clients want the therapist's help in avoiding anxiety, and may therefore resent the cognitive therapist's attempts to elicit anxiety in sessions. Therefore, both individual therapist and client characteristics and the characteristics of the therapy can cause difficulties.

Using Difficulties in the Therapeutic Relationship 'in the Service of Therapy'

Conceptualising and working with difficulties in the therapeutic relationship assumes that these difficulties are a product of the same kind of patterns of thinking, unhelpful assumptions or schemata as are any other difficulties, particularly interpersonal difficulties. Therefore, such problems can be identified, understood and worked with in the same way in cognitive therapy as are the client's presenting problems. The extra factor is that the counsellor's own patterns of thinking, unhelpful assumptions or schemata are also relevant, and need to be conceptualised and worked with. The problems may reflect difficulties in other areas of the client's life, and solving difficulties in the therapeutic relationship may offer the client a means of solving difficulties in other relationships.

A number of stages are involved in working with difficulties in the therapeutic relationship: assessment and weaving the issues into the conceptualisation, then collaboratively sharing and working on the issues with the client. The value and importance of supervision must be stressed when identifying and working with difficulties in the counselling process: because of the nature of the therapeutic relationship, without supervision from others, it is often difficult to even spot that there are potential or actual pitfalls.

Assessment: Becoming a Participant Observer

The first step to working with difficulties in the therapeutic relationship is to identify and assess what is going on (Newman, 1994; Safran and Segal, 1990). Some problems are immediately obvious, for example if the client and counsellor end up 'arguing', or the counsellor feels strongly negative towards the client. However, it can also be very difficult to identify problems or difficulties at the time, since we are by definition a participant in the relationship with the client, and our behaviour will inevitably be affected by the encounter. Both counsellor and client are likely to 'pull' from each other behaviours or emotional responses that will maintain their schemata. Inevitably, the therapist will get sucked in to the client's way of being, leading to a 'dysfunctional cognitive-interpersonal cycle' (Safran, 1990; Safran and Segal, 1990).

Safran and Segal describe a model for both identifying 'rupture markers' when the therapeutic relationship becomes strained or impaired, and intervening, using the context of the therapeutic relationship. The key to assessing difficulties is initially to observe as well as participate in the difficulties. This involves becoming a 'participant observer', using 'decentring' – the process of stepping outside one's immediate experience and thereby not only observing the experience but also changing the nature of the experience itself. Rather than simply being part of and reacting to an encounter, or being 'hooked' into the interaction, such as may happen during conversation outside of therapy, the therapist is also aware of being a participant in the encounter. The therapist then 'unhooks' from the interaction to avoid becoming so engaged in it that client's schemata are, yet again, confirmed (Kiesler, 1988). In psychoanalytic therapy, the process is called developing an 'observing ego' or developing the 'observing self', or developing the 'internal supervisor' (Casement, 1985). In cognitive therapy, this is far from an alien concept: it mirrors what we are constantly asking our clients to do in observing and monitoring their thoughts, affect and behaviour. Completing the Dysfunctional Thoughts Record, for example, involves both acting in the situation and thinking the thoughts, and observing the self thinking and feeling (Teasdale, 1996). During the 'hooked' stage, the individual feels, for example, anxious, thinks anxious thoughts and behaves anxiously. During the 'unhooked' or observing stage, she is able to observe herself being anxious. In the therapy situation, once the interaction is both experienced and observed, it is possible to discuss what is happening and generate hypotheses for the conceptualisation.

The process of hooking and unhooking is illustrated with the client Tony discussed in Chapter 3 (p. 62). Tony had struggled for years with persistent abdominal pains and believed 'No-one is to be trusted'. He was both wanting help from the counsellor and wanting to prove that the counsellor could not help him. During the 'hooked' stage of counselling, the client's behaviour forces the counsellor into a narrow and restricted range of responses: to Tony's questions about his symptoms, the counsellor can only respond by desperately trying to be 'the expert' and answer all his questions. In the unhooked stage, the first task is to 'unhook', and notice, attend to and try to label what is being pulled from the counsellor by the client. The second task involves discontinuing with the usual responses, and discussing what is going on, such as reflecting, 'I feel like I'm being tested to see how much I know: I wonder what went through your mind just before you said x. . . . [W]hat you are feeling right now?' By using this process, gaining supervision and dealing with my own negative reactions, Tony continued counselling and began to look at his mistrust: neither client nor therapist gave up on the other.

Newman (1994) suggests a number of questions that the counsellor can use to assess difficulties. Although it is suggested that the counsellor ask these questions about the client, it is also useful for the counsellor to assess his own role in the difficulties:

- What is the function of the client's behaviour? What does the client fear will happen if the difficulties were not there? For example, being angry with the counsellor may protect the client from other, more painful feelings.
- How do the problems fit with the longitudinal or developmental conceptualisation?
- When and under what circumstances has the client been similarly affected in the past?
- What counsellor or client beliefs are feeding the current situation? How might the client or counsellor be characteristically misunderstanding or misinterpreting the other or the

situation? That is, what schema maintenance behaviours are in operation?

- Does the counsellor or client lack certain skills which make it difficult to collaborate with counselling or resolve the present difficulties? For example, either client or counsellor may have problems with assertiveness which is causing difficulties.
- Are there environmental factors influencing the counselling? For example, the client's partner may fear change, and so may actively block the client's 'homework' assignments.
- Does the conceptualisation need revision? For example, a client who says 'You don't understand' may be right because the counsellor may be overlooking important points because they do not fit with his conceptualisation.

Collaboration

Once difficulties are identified and assessed, counsellor and client work together to conceptualise and deal with the difficulties. The therapist shares her or his thoughts, ideas, conceptualisation or feelings, as appropriate, in the service of collaboratively working with the difficulties. This process must be guided by the conceptualisation, and is both an extremely valuable and potentially 'dangerous' stage of therapy. For example, interventions focusing on the relationship can be extremely threatening to clients who have had no experience of being able to discuss or resolve relationship difficulties. Interventions can be understood in different ways, according to the client's assumptions or schema. For example, the intervention 'I'm getting the feeling that we are not on the same wavelength at the moment: I wonder how you are feeling right now?' may activate a 'No-one understands me' schema, leading to the client walking out of the room, or may elicit the response 'God, this therapist is from another planet – I'll demand to see the boss' from a client with an entitlement schema, or may give rise to a profound sense of relief that it is OK to say 'I don't understand' from a client who believes that 'Feelings aren't OK'. Therefore, grounding the interventions in the conceptualisation is essential. 'Here and now' examples within the session are valuable to explore difficulties, using guided discovery to identify the client's thoughts and feelings at times of 'alliance ruptures'. The counsellor can ask the client: 'When I said x, it looked as though it was uncomfortable: what went through your mind just then?' or 'When I said x, you seemed to close off – was there something about it that was familiar? . . . Have you felt like this before? . . . Did it remind you of something?'

When giving any kind of feedback to clients about what is going on in the relationship, therapists must acknowledge their own contribution to the experience, and not blame or pathologise the client. Rather than saying, 'I feel like you are trying to control the interaction', the therapist can offer her own feelings: 'I feel like I am involved in a struggle with you at the moment. I am not sure what is going on. How does this relate to your feelings right now?' The therapist may wish to say, 'I feel like I am giving you a lecture at the moment, and am not sure why this is so', or 'I feel quite puzzled when you tell me you are sad but laugh at the same time': the therapist's response does not aim to reassure the client, but holds the moment by implying that they can sort out the problem together. Mere reassurance often only glosses over the issue without tackling the underlying beliefs.

Therapy for Therapists
We all know that, at times, difficulties in the therapeutic relationship arise from the therapist and her or his particular experience and psychology. Cognitive therapists such as Layden have recently integrated the concepts of transference and countertransference into cognitive therapy, pointing out the need for cognitive therapists to be congruent in the degree that they as well as their clients, need to be 'open to the evidence' and to the possibility that the therapy may be influenced by their own schemata and countertransference. Layden et al. (1993) describe some of the characteristics of therapists which facilitate work with difficulties in the therapeutic relationship. The therapist needs to be a 'real person', who acts in a consistently positive, supportive manner, maintaining a firm grounding in reality, an even temperament, and being willing to address difficulties in the therapeutic relationship as they occur. The therapist must be secure enough in himself to admit to mistakes, and have non-judgemental self-awareness. Although this list may read as an advert for 'Therapist Dateline', and activate the therapist's inadequacy and helplessness schema, Layden et al. (1993) operationalise it in terms of questions the therapist can ask himself before offering interventions at the level of the therapeutic relationship: 'How will my patient benefit from this intervention' and 'How will I benefit from this intervention?' If the answer to the latter is more apparent than the answer to the former, the intervention should be

postponed and reflected on, by self-reflection and supervision. The cognitive approaches described in this book, such as thought diaries and downward arrow techniques, can be very usefully applied to ourselves, to identify and resolve the therapist's reactions to the client or the process of therapy (Freeman et al., 1990; Layden et al., 1993; Persons, 1989; Wright and Davis, 1994). Such techniques can also help the therapist to identify his assumptions and beliefs that may underlie reactions to the client, in particular the therapist's 'shoulds' (Persons, 1989). For example, if the therapist feels angry when the patient reports a setback after doing well in therapy, he may identify thoughts and assumptions such as 'The patient should be getting better by now: this must mean I'm doing a lousy job, and if I'm found out, I'll lose my job'. Key phrases can help the therapist deal with these situations: for example, 'This is her stuff, I won't take it personally' enables us to observe a client's extreme negative reactions, such as anger and rage, as directed at the therapist rather than letting it in and activating our own schema. Therapy tapes can be very useful to identify negative thoughts or other reactions to clients (for example, Wright and Davis, 1994). Other techniques are cognitive rehearsal and role play in supervision to anticipate and work with difficulties in sessions.

Weaving the issues into the conceptualisation is a powerful means of dealing with the therapist's own negative reactions to the client. It can be helpful to ask oneself 'If I had this background and set of beliefs, how would I be feeling or thinking in response to x?' For example, I (DS) found myself feeling annoyed and hostile towards a 56-year-old male client as he described his anger towards his wife who had asked to go and visit their daughter and leave him alone for a weekend. My own thoughts were 'Selfish pig . . . she's devoted herself to looking after you for all these years, why can't she have some time off?' Putting myself in his shoes, having been looked after all these years made the prospect of being on his own and negotiating domestic tasks extremely frightening. Putting my principles aside, I could empathise with his anger and fear.

Conclusion

We have, in this chapter, given a flavour of the difficulties which may arise in cognitive therapy and a flavour of the way in which a cognitive therapist might set about solving such difficulties. Some arise from the tasks and methods of cognitive therapy; other issues, to do with the interpersonal nature of the encounter, are likely to be familiar across all therapies. The philosophy behind problem resolution may be expressed as Occam's razor: *Entia non sunt multiplicanda praeter necessitatem*, or, for non Latin-speakers, 'Entities ought not to be multiplied except from necessity'. Translated into cognitive therapy terms, this means the best solution is one that gives the most benefit for the least effort, and therefore the simplest. We have stressed the importance of a 'bottom-up' approach to dealing with difficulties, and the importance of collaboration at whatever level the difficulties occur. At times this means acknowledging our own contribution to the encounter: in the words of Albert Ellis (Dryden, 1991), being willing to be a 'fucked up, fallible' human being at times of dealing with difficulties is essential. If the therapist is able to be 'real' and admit to mistakes or uncertainties, this can be both a powerful model and a means of challenging assumptions or schemata within sessions.

8
Ending Cognitive Therapy and Long-Term Coping

Cognitive therapy is, frequently, a structured time-limited therapy, focusing on the goals that the client brings to therapy, and the success, or otherwise, in meeting those goals. Cognitive therapy has a reputation for being a short-term therapy, and it has been criticised as therefore not getting to the root of the problems or leaving the client stranded at the end. We have hoped to address some of these criticisms throughout the book, and, in this chapter, look at the issues surrounding ending therapy, and making sure that the client neither feels that her core difficulties have not been solved, nor feels left high and dry at the end of therapy. We discuss assessing when therapy is to end, stages of ending, the value of offering follow-up sessions, and helping clients to prepare for future difficulties and prepare a 'blueprint' for long-term coping. We also look at what happens when endings do not go according to plan: when the client abruptly terminates or disappears, when the client does not feel any better at the end of therapy, or when other unresolved issues get in the way of a satisfactory ending.

Endings in Cognitive Therapy

Beck originally developed cognitive therapy for depression to be conducted over 12 to 20 sessions, and research evidence has shown that the therapy can be, and often is, very effective in this kind of time frame. This relatively short-term aspect has made the cognitive approach a popular one where time and resources are under particular constraints: for example, therapy settings within the Health Service. No doubt, also, the brief nature of cognitive therapy means that client and therapist are more likely to work parsimoniously and efficiently: 'Being under sentence of termination doth most marvellously concentrate the material' (quoted in

Dryden and Feltham, 1992, p. 159). A short time frame would normally allow for full work at the 'bottom end': that is, symptom and automatic thought level. It should also allow a certain amount of assumption- and, even, schema-level work, depending on the kinds and length of problems the client brings to therapy. However, a short time frame would probably only allow a certain amount of working through at the 'top end' of the formulation, and normally major assumption and/or schema work is held to take considerably longer periods of therapy. For example, if a client's main goal is to get rid of panic attacks, then short-term work can be effective, and both help the client with the presenting problem, and, directly or indirectly, begin to challenge the client's beliefs or improve self-esteem. If the client has long-term, enduring difficulties in many areas of life, although a lot of good work can be done in short-term therapy, it is probably necessary to work at the level of schema, thereby necessitating longer therapy.

Whether short-term or long-term work is needed can to some extent be estimated during the assessment phase of the work and taken into account when setting goals. Ending therapy is therefore a phase of therapy that, in fact, starts right at the beginning when negotiating a contract with the client. During goal-setting, the topic of ending is noted, for example by asking the client to think about questions such as 'How will your life be different once counselling is finished?', and 'How will we know when we've finished?' Commonly, the therapist gives the client an exact number of sessions that are available: something in the region of 6 to 10 for anxiety, 10 to 15 for depression, and so on. Whether the therapy is likely to last one month or one or two years, it is important to be explicit about the dates the therapy will be reviewed, as well as being explicit about the possible time scale of therapy and therefore about the ending. Both client and counsellor need frequent reminders of where the therapy has got to, looking back to progress made and forward to future sessions. Sometimes it is helpful to remind the client how many sessions are left at every session; sometimes incorporating reviews every few sessions serves as a reminder without appearing overly number-crunching. Whatever the number of sessions, frequent reviews every six sessions or so enable client and therapist to check that they are on course.

Another important characteristic of cognitive therapy is that it aims to help the client to become his own therapist, teaching clients ways of helping themselves, across a number of situations or problems. Although, when working as any form of therapist, our clients are the centre of our professional lives, the therapy may not be so central to the client's life, and learning goes on apart from and after the sessions (Budman and Gurman, 1988). As stated by Judith Beck, 'A therapist who views himself as responsible for helping the patient with every problem risks engendering or reinforcing dependence and deprives the patient of the opportunity to test and strengthen her skills' (1995, p. 269). One of the key advantages of the cognitive approach is its ability to generalise, or transfer the benefits, from work during therapy to post-therapy. Such generalising can be a major factor in preventing relapse. The message throughout therapy is that the real work is a function of what goes on between sessions as well as within sessions, expressed as a concentration on homework and generalising therapeutic gains across different situations. Thus the cognitive approach seems to have a key advantage in helping to militate against 'wash out' of gains over time – a phenomenon which is, in fact, a distressingly common outcome for many forms of therapy (Ivey et al., 1987). Therefore, ending therapy is concerned with what the client has learned and how the client will, in future, cope with various different situations or difficulties. Leading on from this 'learning' function of cognitive therapy are the ways in which ending therapy might be extremely difficult for some clients: those whose hopelessness prevents them from being able to generalise from sessions; those with issues of dependence believing themselves incapable of disengaging from the therapist and coping alone. Thus, the stage of ending, as for other stages of therapy, requires both identification of and working through many of the key issues for the client.

The Process of Ending

The ending of counselling in general, and cognitive therapy in particular, is an important issue which seems to be surprisingly under-discussed in the literature. Safran and Segal (1990) and Judith Beck (1995) are two sources which we have found helpful. Beck et al. pertinently remind us of the importance of handling endings well: 'Because cognitive therapy is time-limited, the problems associated with termination are usually not as complex as those associated with longer forms of treatment. However, much of the benefit of cognitive therapy can be lost through inappropriate or inept closure' (1979, p. 317). One way of understanding the end of cognitive therapy is to conceptualise it as a process or stage which needs to be given an appropriate amount of time and attention, rather than a sudden cessation of activity (Ward, 1989). In the words of Yalom, 'Termination is more than an act signifying the end of therapy; it is an integral part of the process of therapy and, if properly understood and managed, may be an important factor in the instigation of change' (1975, p. 365).

Having a good conceptualisation of the client's beliefs and assumptions is invaluable in predicting and working with difficulties in ending counselling. On approaching ending, the therapist can ask herself 'What does this client's conceptualisation tell me about how the client is likely to see ending?' The client's response to ending can be identified and worked with in a collaborative way, and be seen as the opportunity for one last piece of, perhaps crucial, therapeutic learning. For example, schemata concerned with dependency on others or beliefs that the client is unable to cope alone are likely to be activated during the ending of counselling, particularly if the client and counsellor have formed a good therapeutic relationship. For other clients, where counselling has been less helpful, beliefs may be activated and strengthened such as 'No-one can help me'. If such issues have already emerged, as we suppose they should have done in good therapy, then they will have been incorporated into the conceptualisation and thus will have shown themselves in attempts to predict the course of therapy. For some clients, these predictions can be very valuable as they allow the therapist to offer the client the chance to make a deliberate good end to the therapy. This, having been an elusive experience for them in other types of relationships, can therefore prove to be a very valuable learning experience and an excellent end to the therapy.

Ending counselling may involve three stages (Ward, 1989). The first stage involves assessing the client's readiness for the end of therapy. The second stage involves addressing and resolving remaining issues and bringing about appropriate closure of the relationship between client and counsellor. The third stage enables the client to consolidate what has been gained and learned during counselling and carry on using these gains after counselling has ended. The extent to which each of these three stages is emphasised depends on the individual client and the counselling situation.

Assessing When to End Cognitive Therapy
The usual criteria for when to stop counselling are when the client feels better about the presenting problems and is acting differently in life, or at least working in that direction. The client's goals for counselling and the extent to which they have been met need to be the main factors guiding the end of counselling. The simplest, and most collaborative, way of assessing when to end therapy is to ask the client. For many, if not the majority, of our clients, their main aim is to get better and get on with their lives. They are the best judge of when they are able to meet that aim. However, it is important that the goals set by both client and therapist are realistic. Therapy is not likely to resolve all problems, remove all symptoms or result in a 'complete cure', and clients may well still experience the symptoms that led them to seek help in the first place. It is also not realistic for the client to expect never to feel anxious, low, upset or angry again: therefore an important goal of therapy is to be able to normalise his distress. This may be particularly important for clients who have not been able to express or experience emotional distress, who may be feeling significantly more emotionally fluid since starting counselling, perhaps feeling and expressing emotions in a way which was previously uncharacteristic of the individual.

When counselling ends may well be fixed by practical constraints caused by factors external to the client and counsellor. Particularly when working in the Health Service and educational settings, the number of counselling sessions it is possible to offer a client is limited, often to 6 to 10 sessions for short-term work or 20 sessions for longer-term work. Working within a limited number of sessions helps the counselling maintain a structure and focus, helps to make the best use of the available time, and may give the client the important message that the problems are manageable and solutions can be found in a relatively brief period of time. However, such limits may also mean that important issues can only be touched upon and are not fully addressed. Whatever the length of counselling, the limit is discussed and negotiated during the first session. As we have discussed above, the stage of ending is therefore introduced and to some extent planned right at the beginning.

When to begin to discuss ending with the client depends to

some extent on the individual client. We have discussed how it is important to be clear with the client at all stages how many sessions are available and how many are left; however, it is not necessarily helpful to be constantly reminded of endings when the client is very distressed, or in the middle of working through very difficult issues. For other clients, reminders of the ending can increase their hopefulness about progress, confirming that their problems are manageable and that professional help is not a life-sentence. We may also find ourselves avoiding bringing up the subject of ending, a situation related perhaps to the client's fears about ending or dependency on the therapist, or the therapist's issues about endings.

One way of beginning the end of counselling is to begin to increase the time between sessions. The counsellor and client may meet weekly during the initial stages of counselling, but may then spread out the sessions to every two or three weeks. In addition, clients are encouraged to see the therapist for follow-up sessions approximately 3, 6 and 12 months after ending. Spacing sessions in this way enables the client to have more time between sessions in which to practise and consolidate gains made during counselling, and also allows any potential difficulties to arise before counselling has ended.

Dealing with Unresolved Issues and Ending the Therapeutic Relationship

During the final stages of cognitive therapy, the client may well identify issues that have not been resolved during previous sessions. It is important that the client and counsellor collaboratively discuss how best to deal with these issues. It may be possible to negotiate a number of additional sessions; it may be more appropriate to look for other sources of help such as relationship counselling. Some clients may bring important issues to the last session, with the flavour of a 'parting shot', leaving the counsellor puzzled, frustrated or annoyed, which may mean therapy ends with an unfinished feeling. It may be that these issues are too difficult or threatening for the client to work with them; they may be brought up as a way of continuing the therapeutic relationship. It is important to try to discuss what has happened and offer some understanding in terms of the client's conceptualisation.

The end of the counselling relationship may evoke a variety of feelings including loss, grief or abandonment. Safran and Segal

(1990) note that ending therapy can activate specific interpersonal schemata, such as those of abandonment and dependence. Addressing and discussing these feelings is an important part of the stage of ending counselling, enabling the client's reactions to be understood as part of the overall conceptualisation. The client can be encouraged to look at any similarities between ending counselling and other endings. The client can be invited to think about how she usually handles saying good-bye, and whether she wishes to try out a different, more satisfactory way of ending the relationship, as the following example illustrates.

> Joanna found ending any relationship extremely difficult, her feelings evoked in saying good-bye being almost unbearable. She tended to always leave without saying good-bye, promising to get in touch before a friend left and then not contacting her, leaving relationships at the first sign that things may be going wrong. Her beliefs included 'People always abandon me eventually'; 'There's no point in saying good-bye: they'll go anyway'. Her way of coping with endings avoided the pain of confronting her loss, but led to great dissatisfaction and a feeling of something missing. Towards the end of the allocated time, Joanna, predictably, started to cancel or not to attend appointments. Although, given the pressures in the NHS to discharge people who do not attend a certain number of appointments, I (DS) was tempted to give up on Joanna, thus confirming her beliefs, but I persisted in contacting her after a missed appointment to offer her another. When she eventually came back, we were able to identify her feelings around ending her sessions, and identify ways in which she could try out a different approach to ending with me. We both worked out a way to say a more satisfactory 'good-bye'.

The process of ending cognitive therapy also seeks to remind the client of the ways in which he is responsible for changes (J. Beck, 1995). A client who says 'If it wasn't for you . . .' or 'You've made me so much better' may give the therapist a warm, self-satisfied glow, but should be used not to boost the therapist's self-esteem but as an opportunity to attribute progress to the client. For example, a response to such praise might be to ask the client the proportion of the work in therapy done by the client versus therapist, the amount of time the client has been tackling the problems (24 hours a day, 7 days a week) versus the amount of time the therapist has put in (10 hours). Dismissing their own contribution to therapy may relate to the client's beliefs around dependency or powerlessness: therefore, the ending can be used to enable him to develop alternative beliefs. Another response to ending therapy may be for the client to feel angry about the need to seek 'professional help' in the first place. Although such a response to coming for help is often looked at during the early stages of therapy, sometimes the client may have found the process of therapy to have made sense in a way that leads him to question 'Why couldn't I do it for myself?' Such responses, as for other responses to ending therapy, need careful attention.

The ending of counselling is a stage for the counsellor as well as the client. It is important for us, too, to look at our feelings at ending counselling. If the counsellor has found the client particularly difficult to work with, or counselling has not been particularly helpful, she may feel a sense of disappointment at not being able to help or relief at finishing with the client. Alternatively, sometimes it is difficult for us to end counselling at the point at which the client is improving or becoming more emotionally accessible and therefore more rewarding to work with. An example is given below.

> Paul presented with quite severe difficulties at work and in his marriage. During his first session, he was angry at 'having' to see me (DS), did not think there was any point in just talking about things, and simply wanted a prescription for Prozac. At the end of the first session, he reported that despite his misgivings he had found talking helpful, and was a bit more hopeful that he could sort things out. He turned out to be an easy and rewarding client to work with: he took to the cognitive model with ease, devouring the recommended self-help books, and began to make long-overdue changes to his life. He was able to make use of the depression, looking back and seeing it as a valuable indicator that he needed to take stock. I felt sad at ending therapy with him, partly because he represented an 'easy' case amongst a sea of more complex clients, and partly because, on reflection, I realised that some of the issues he was successfully tackling, with the flavour of a 'mid-life crisis', were those that I, too, felt were close to my own issues.

Colarusso and Nemiroff (1981) note how it can often be useful to look at the intermeshing of the client's developmental stage with one's own, as illustrated above. The therapist's feelings, both positive and negative, are often best dealt with during supervision, giving an opportunity to end the therapy successfully for the therapist as well as for the client.

Preparing for the Future: Long-Term Coping

As therapist and client begin to reach the end of therapy, they begin to review the progress that has been made in the therapy and what implications the gains or lack of gains have for the ending of therapy. Cognitive therapy, as we have discussed, stresses the active and self-help nature of the therapy. To a large extent, the therapy moves from more activity on the part of the therapist at the early stages, to more activity on the part of the client later on. Handing over the reins of therapy is completed at the end stages. Ideally, the client will have practised new ways of seeing situations, new ways of thinking or new ways of acting in different situations, promoting the generalisability of therapy. Clients often need concrete reminders of progress. The pen-and-paper nature of the therapy enables the clients to collect written information throughout the therapy; flashcards with specific information or ways of seeing things give the client instant reminders of key points during the therapy. A therapy flashcard is shown in Figure 8.1.

In order to ensure the generalisability of therapy, client and therapist can work together to assess, firstly, whether the client is ready to end, and, secondly, how to cope in the face of future difficulties. The client may have doubts about ending counselling or may want to end therapy 'early', when important issues are left dangling. The client may 'give up' on therapy before giving it a

---

Reminder of what I have learned:

There are times when I'm anxious, but try to swim along with it: nothing awful is going to happen.

I've been anxious many times and it's felt like something bad is going to happen, but it never has.

Even if I feel anxious and sick, I'm not going to be sick.

Even if I did feel very ill, it would not be a complete disaster: other people would help.

Remember, the more I think about how anxious I feel, the more anxious I feel. Try to keep my mind off it. Pay attention to something else. Carry on as normal.

Don't get out of the habit of doing things – keep going despite how I feel. Make friends even if it is a bit frightening.

I KNOW I CAN DO THINGS
DON'T DWELL ON HOW I FEEL ALL THE TIME
DON'T DWELL ON EVEN THE SLIGHTEST MISTAKE I'VE MADE
IMAGINE PUTTING ALL THE WORRIES IN MY HEAD IN A RUBBISH BIN.

Figure 8.1   *Therapy flashcard*

good try. In this case, therapist and client can work out the pros and cons of both ending therapy and continuing (J. Beck, 1995) in order, collaboratively, to arrive at a decision. Towards the end of counselling, the counsellor can act as 'devil's advocate' for the client: the client can put forward the arguments in favour of ending counselling and how to cope in future, and the counsellor can attempt to challenge these, to help the client clarify possible issues in ending counselling. Dryden (1982) describes the use of 'rational role reversal': the client becomes the therapist, and the therapist the client. As 'client', you describe your difficulties and negative thinking, which the 'therapist' then aims to challenge and work with. Alternatively, the client may develop an image of the counsellor or other helper sitting on her shoulder and talking to her whenever she experiences difficulties, effectively acting as a 'transitional object' (Dryden and Feltham, 1992). One of my (DS) clients reported that he was able to conjure up an image of me as an owl offering him different ways of seeing things: related not, as I initially presumed, to my great wisdom, but to the large glasses which I used to wear.

As we have stressed throughout the book, cognitive therapy aims to help the client to learn approaches that can be applied across many different situations. Successful therapy does not, unfortunately, mean the client will never again have problems. Both therapist and client may, however, be reluctant to bring up the thorny issue of what happens if things go wrong: the therapist wanting to engender hope, and the client preferring not to think about future problems. Progress is, however, rarely in a straight line, and some form of setback is common. Setback does not necessarily mean relapse; relapse does not necessarily mean that the client is back to square one. It can be very helpful to explain to clients the model of change advocated by Prochaska and DiClemente (1984), where change moves from precontemplation, contemplation, action to maintenance. In its simplest form, when tackling problems, we tend to move around in a circle, firstly not even being aware of the problem (precontemplation), to recognising that there is a problem (contemplation), to doing something about it (action) and keeping up progress (maintenance). Should the client start to experience problems, rather than viewing them as back to square one, it can be helpful to look at ways she can get back on to the cycle, identifying the need for change and what to do in order to change.

In order to promote maintenance, the client may need concrete reminders of what to do in case of difficulties. During the process of ending therapy, the client can be asked to work on a 'blueprint', or first aid book, of how beneficial change will be maintained and how future problems may be handled. This process is described by Judith Beck:

> The therapist encourages the patient to read through and organise all her therapy notes so she can easily refer to them in future. For homework, she may write a synopsis of the important points and skills she has learned in therapy and review this list with the therapist. . . . [T]he therapist prepares the client for setbacks early in treatment. Nearing termination, the therapist encourages the patient to compose a coping card specifying what to do if a setback occurs after therapy has ended. (1995, p. 278)

Working on a blueprint involves at least two sessions for the client to think about the questions and work through them with the counsellor. An example of a completed blueprint is given in Figure 8.2.

The stages of working on a blueprint involve inviting the client to think about what kind of difficulties of her own, in others or in her situation, may be encountered in future. What kind of problems led up to the client requesting help? Is it likely that these problems will recur? If so, what can be done? What are the early signs of problems? Who else may be able to help? The client can be encouraged to carry on after counselling has ended working on the issues identified during counselling. An important goal is for the client to become her own therapist, or be able to use informal support networks rather than automatically relying on professional help. An example of a 'self-therapy' session is given by Judith Beck (1995), where the client can set aside time to conduct a session with herself, incorporating the usual structure of agenda, reviews, and so on.

OFFERING FOLLOW-UP SESSIONS   Many counsellors will routinely offer clients one or more follow-up sessions after counselling has ended in which to review progress and work on difficulties. Offering follow-up sessions may be valuable, particularly for those clients with long-term difficulties or personality disorders. Therapist and client need to decide whether to arrange regular reviews, regardless of how the client is feeling, or more open access, that is, the client is able to contact the therapist for emergency sessions. However, continuing contact with the

What have I learned?	Modifying my thoughts can change my feelings. I don't necessarily need tablets. I can challenge my thoughts.
How can I build on this? What's my Plan for Action?	I can define how I want to be: more light-hearted. I can learn to worry less. I can actively plan more enjoyable activities: go to the cinema; go for walks at weekends.
What will make it difficult for me to put this Plan for Action into practice?	Taking work home. Not going to work feeling fresh. Getting into a cycle of 'no time', 'no motivation'.
How will I deal with these difficulties?	Keep on reviewing the costs and benefits of positive and negative actions and thoughts.
What might lead to a setback? e.g. Stresses, life problems, relationships, etc.	Problems at work. Ill health.
If I do have a setback, what will I do about it?	Seek help early from family and friends, GP, counsellor. Read the self-help books.

Figure 8.2   *Cognitive therapy blueprint*

counsellor may be a means of the client or counsellor avoiding saying good-bye and dealing with the resulting feelings of loss, or avoiding issues of dependency. It is important for the client and counsellor to be aware of the hazards as well as potential benefits of offering follow-up sessions.

Sudden Endings

The progression of therapy from beginning, middle to end often involves satisfactory completion of each of those stages. However, we have all had the experience of clients who suddenly terminate therapy, leaving a sense of incompletion for the therapist and uncertainty about 'where we went wrong'. Such feelings indicate that there is some kind of ideal way for counselling to end, contravened by the client who just disappears. Sudden endings imply that the client has ended before the therapist thinks they 'should' (Dryden and Feltham, 1992). There is some evidence that shows that clients consistently seem to want to finish counselling before the therapist, and many examples of where the client feels 'coerced' into carrying on with therapy against their wishes (Dryden and Feltham, 1992). However, cognitive approaches stress that the ideal way of ending has to be conceptualised and operationalised for the individual client. In a truly collaborative relationship, the client's wishes regarding termination are those on which decisions are made: thus, if the client wants to end, the therapist respects this decision and is able to deal with his own issues accordingly. The client's wishes to end therapy can be openly discussed, the pros and cons of ending weighed up, the therapist encouraging the client to be open about feedback to him. Should the therapist want to carry on where the client wishes to end, it is possible that client and therapist are working from different conceptualisations: the therapist may believe that schema-driven issues are at the root of the problems and need working on before ending, the client being happy to feel a bit better and get back to 'coping'. The client's conceptualisation can be used as a way of approaching sudden endings: for example, the client who has learned not to trust people, developing the belief 'No-one can really help you anyway', is likely to translate whatever happens in therapy in terms of the belief; thus, one difficult or unproductive session may lead to schema-confirmation and the end of therapy. The desire to end therapy can, ideally, be both understood and handled using the case conceptualisation.

The 'sudden death' kind of ending requires careful handling. When clients simply disappear, we need to think about our responsibilities to follow up these people. Again, returning to the client's conceptualisation, 'walking in their shoes' and carefully discussing and reviewing previous sessions may help us to understand what is going on. Sudden ending may be a way of the client coping with the ending, or may be a way of her communicating with the therapist, as in the example of Joanna above. The client may be acting out interpersonal strategies, part of which may be to suddenly disappear only to suddenly reappear later on. Whether or not we take the active step of contacting the client may depend on the particular issues for him. For example, following the disappearance of a client who believed 'Nobody really cares about me', the decision to pursue him was well justified by his successful re-entry into counselling.

Relapse Prevention

Cognitive therapy has focused on relapse prevention for many psychological problems, and the evidence suggests that relapse following cognitive therapy is lower than following other forms of therapy or pharmacotherapy (Evans et al., 1992; Shea et al., 1992). As discussed above, the ending stage of therapy involves looking at what might happen should the client feel he is going back to square one, or seemingly insurmountable difficulties begin to arise. It is likely that relapse is associated with re-emergence of schema issues following successful work with the client's presenting problems such as depression. One way of conceptualising relapse prevention for these clients is enabling the client to view his difficulties as equivalent to chronic conditions such as diabetes, which, when looked after properly, have less impact on the individual's life than when ignored. A car analogy may be helpful: the yellow light indicates that the oil is seriously low, but it is more helpful to check and top up the oil on a regular basis than to only use the warning sign. Similarly, if the client is prone to react in a certain way when particular schemata are triggered, and therefore remain vulnerable to relapse, regular maintenance is crucial. Such maintenance may be in the form of regular booster sessions, regular self-reviews by the client, and learning to identify the early warning signals and respond quickly rather than waiting until a serious problem develops.

What Happens When Resources Do Not Meet Demand?

It used to be common lore in the counselling and psychotherapy worlds that most if not all of our clients are in need of long-term therapy. Even if a small number of sessions begin to resolve the problems clients bring into therapy, underlying issues are likely to catch the client out in future, and therefore require addressing. However, a combination of research evidence and pragmatism is challenging such a view. We have discussed throughout the book how the parsimonious approach of cognitive therapy enables much work to be done in a relatively short space of time, and standard brief cognitive therapy may be helpful for many of our clients (Clark and Fairburn, 1996): although we may identify issues but not address them, it seems as if these can be safely left alone for many people. Recent work in Oxford has shown that for clients with no 'personality disorder', as assessed by the therapist's clinical impressions, limiting the number of sessions to a maximum of 10, regardless of the client's problems, is as effective as offering a larger number of sessions (Westbrook, 1993), a finding which may make both purchasers and providers sigh with relief.

Limitations in resources are increasingly dictating how many sessions we are able to offer, particularly in the NHS and educational settings. As a result, even those who might benefit from brief therapy may not be offered sufficient help, and resources may not be available to offer clients the number of sessions indicated for those people needing longer therapy. We are not able, here, to offer any words of wisdom to solve the gnawing problem of limited resources, particularly working in the public sector; however, the self-help nature of cognitive therapy means that many of our clients may benefit from one or two assessment sessions and guidance towards one or more of the many excellent self-help cognitive therapy books on the market (for example, Blackburn, 1987; Burns, 1980, 1989; Butler and Hope, 1996; Greenberger and Padesky, 1995). Whilst cognitive therapy developed as an individual therapy, there has been interest in its application to group settings. Scott and Stradling (1990) showed that group and individual therapy were equally effective in terms of amount of change per client, with the group therapy being significantly more efficient in terms of resources. Clients may well do best in a therapy format that most closely matches their personality: for example, clients whose identity is bound up with achievement may do best in individual therapy, whilst those needing the approval of others may do best in groups (Zettle et al., 1992).

Conclusion

The end of cognitive therapy is a stage which starts right at the beginning and ends throughout the process of follow-up sessions. Ideally the ending of the meetings between therapist and client is not an end of therapy, since the aim is for the client to become her own therapist, and be able to generalise learning to other situations or problems. The learning associated with ending therapy works both ways: ending with each of our clients gives us the opportunity to reflect on the work that we did, to reflect on the conceptualisation of the particular client we developed and evolved, and, most importantly, to reflect how we might consolidate or change our practice as a result of the journey with each individual. Blueprinting and relapse prevention are for both client and therapist.

PART III
COGNITIVE THERAPY FOR COUNSELLORS

9

Cognitive Approaches and Counselling

For much of its history, counselling has been strongly influenced by humanistic and psychodynamic approaches. Behaviourism has been particularly unpopular, and most counsellors would have sided with Carl Rogers in his famous debate with B.F. Skinner (Kirschenbaum and Henderson, 1990). In contrast, the cognitive therapies have traditionally been more popular amongst psychologists and psychiatrists than amongst counsellors. As a result, cognitive approaches have tended to be under-taught on counselling courses. Where they have been taught, they have probably been covered with less knowledge and enthusiasm than that applied to other approaches.

We hope that we have so far shown enough of the strong and ongoing developmental movement within cognitive therapy to encourage many counsellors to think that there may be more to be taken from the discipline than they had previously realised. In line with the general development of integrative and eclectic approaches in counselling and psychotherapy (Dryden, 1992), there are now new spaces and opportunities for counsellors to make increasing use of cognitive perspectives. One difficulty for trainee counsellors of all kinds is to know how to begin to practise new skills and techniques when they feel they have little expertise in them. Should one dip a toe in the shallow end, plunge into the deep end, or start somewhere in the middle? In this chapter, we offer our personal reflections on the issues faced by counsellors who are interested in pursuing cognitive methods. We look at how to match the type of therapy with the type of therapist and the therapy situation, and discuss whether cognitive approaches best suit certain counsellors, or certain therapy situations, more than others. We then go on to discuss three levels of applying cognitive methods in counselling, moving through selecting and using techniques in an eclectic way, to a wholehearted commitment to cognitive therapy, and, finally, integrating cognitive approaches with other psychotherapies.

Counselling Training and Cognitive Therapy

From our training experience, we have come to believe that many developing counsellors seem to go down well-trodden pathways. The initial routes are those of counselling skills with most of the milestones carved by Rogers or Egan. These skills help counsellors and therapists to become very good at helping people to tell their stories. Without a wider theoretical understanding, however, it becomes very difficult to make much sense of the stories, especially the more esoteric ones. The path-follower, therefore, begins to collect a variety of theoretical concepts, such as psychodynamic ideas about transference and defence mechanisms, Gestalt experiential techniques and, less commonly, some good cognitive skills such as challenging negative thinking. At this stage the trainee seems to regard such eclecticism with unease, perhaps making it something of a 'dog's breakfast'! Many trainees exit the highway at this stage, perhaps to return to the search later. Those who go on and those who return later often seem to pursue a more single-minded or specialised approach – doing further training in working with a particular theoretical approach or particular client group. Beyond such a specialised training, there are an increasing number of senior practitioners who explore sophisticated, higher-level integrationist approaches.

There is very little research on the natural history of counsellors, and how they develop their style over the years. We have odd pieces of research and fragmentary personal anecdotes from individual counsellors. Two of the stories that I (FW), as a trainer, hear quite frequently are, firstly, 'I tried it with x and it didn't work. Therefore, I'm not going to try it again', and, secondly, 'I tried it with y and it worked! [NB: there is always an exclamation mark here!] . . . Therefore, it's the best thing since sliced bread'. The problem with both of these types of 'informal eclectic experiment' experiences is that they do not give a fair test of the model. The main educational problem with eclecticism is that it is hard to learn anything thoroughly if we are continually experimenting with bits and pieces of methods and theories. This is presumably why the British Association for Counselling and the Counselling Psychology Division of the British Psychological Society have stressed the importance of a core theoretical model in their pronouncements on training. (They do allow for the legitimacy of integrated or eclectic core models but, for example, the course recognition procedures do seem to ask more of them.) Whilst clearness about one's model is obviously admirable, it could also be argued that any training over-focused on only one approach would be somewhat myopic or narrow-minded and would not give the trainee easy access to key debates in the field of counselling and therapy. It is inevitable, therefore, that most training courses will at least touch on theoretical concepts other than those of its core model and that trainees may decide to follow up on them either during the time of the course or later – thus strengthening the idea of informed choice of model.

Matching the Model to the Counsellor
At all levels of training, counsellors may consider the question of what counselling approach to pursue. The counsellor will usually begin by matching a particular concept or technique to the perception of his own style. We make the rationalistic assumption that we choose theoretical orientations according to our basic temperament. This assumption may be an over-simplified notion and there often appears to be more than a hint of the opposite in the equation. For example, I (FW) believe that there is a strong resonance within my 'softish' personality towards the Rogerian approach. Indeed, this was where my initial counselling orientation was located. However, as soon as I began to hear about the cognitive approach in the early 1980s, it pulled strongly on a more focused part of me, working as a compensating mechanism which helps me to avoid becoming too sloppily Rogerian. I like to think that Carl would have understood this. Some person-centred counsellors may have more than a little streak of authoritarianism in them. Several have been insightful and courageous enough to own this – as one put it to me, 'I use person-centredness to put the brakes on Big Brother in me'.

Matching the Model to the Counselling Situation

Apart from personal elements – both those which match and those which balance personal inclinations – other factors in the choice of a model are likely to be the influence of the type of client group worked with and of the type of setting worked in. Cognitive therapies arose from, and continue to be influential in, psychiatric and medical settings. Many of the features of cognitive therapy, such as its short-term focus, the emphasis on evaluation and monitoring and the emphasis on initial symptom relief, have a particularly good fit with these type of settings.

Another feature of cognitive therapy which makes it highly suited to medical and psychiatric settings is the focus on recognisable problem areas such as depression, anxiety and now wider areas such as obsessive-compulsive conditions, post-traumatic stress and personality difficulties. However, this very focus on recognisable problems may be problematic for counsellors. Psychiatric terms can be a difficult block for counsellors to overcome, having traditionally been sceptical of labels and drawn to non-stigmatising and non-judgemental ways of working with people. This reluctance may at times have resulted in less clarity about the focus of work with clients. For example, a depressed client may present with any kind of difficulty such as with relationships or work, but the counsellor will be working with one hand tied behind her back if she is not able to recognise the depression and trace its influence on the presenting problems and then, crucially, target some interventions onto it.

Our experience is that, when the recognition of the depression is skilfully handled by the counsellor, it is experienced not as stigmatising but rather with a sense of relief: 'At last, here is something that can make sense of my experience.' It has always been Beck's strong desire to de-stigmatise many of the so-called 'psychiatric' conditions, motivated by the desire to take what clients had to say about the condition seriously and not to undermine it by labelling it as driven by 'unconscious factors' or 'conditioning' (Beck, 1976). This motivation has held right up to his most recent publications in which he has been speculating on the evolutionary influences on our psychological functioning – so that certain strategies may be normal parts of all our repertoires but over-applied by most of us at some time (Beck, 1996).

Finding Out if the Approach is for You
This is still much for us all to learn, both as individuals and as a profession, about choice of orientation. One approach might be to try different aspects of different approaches and see which of them stick in one's repertoire. The downside of such a strategy, however, is that in order to try to give therapeutic skills a sufficient trial, one may have to persist with them for some time. Persistence is especially required if the skills lie on the therapeutic end of the counselling/therapy continuum. In short, it may be hard to get really good at anything if one is continually trying different skills. At some stage, it may be necessary to give a concentrated range of skills a period of commitment. This commitment may to some extent preclude – at least for a while – developing others. To some degree, most counsellors seem to follow both of these strategies – mixing and matching skills and techniques and following up closely on single theory approaches. Sometimes these two strategies are pursued at the same time whilst, at other times, they are pursued serially. We may all be rather more open to passing influences than we like to think we are. As one family therapist said a few years back, 'You can always tell when Sal Minuchin has been in town. For the next three weeks hundreds of mini Sal Minuchins seem to keep popping up in every clinic you visit.'

Applying Cognitive Approaches to Counselling

With the above ideas about choosing a therapeutic stance in mind, we now turn to issues for counsellors who aspire to use some or all of the concepts described in this book. We describe three levels of application: firstly, using cognitive skills and concepts in a highly eclectic way; secondly, seeking a full training in cognitive therapy, aiming to implement a largely cognitive approach; and thirdly, integration of cognitive skills and concepts with other theoretical approaches.

Level One – Technical Eclectic Use of Cognitive Skills and Concepts
The developing counsellor's first serious brush with cognitive ideas is likely to be Albert Ellis's ABC method or Aaron Beck's concept of automatic thoughts. Once counsellors have grasped the concept of the negative automatic thought or of its rational-

emotive-behaviour therapy equivalents such as 'awfulising' or 'catastrophising', it seems to be a common experience that the counsellor starts to hear them very frequently – not only from clients but also from people in general, including from oneself. Recognising negative thoughts is further enhanced by the recognition of characteristic cognitive themes such as that of loss and sadness in depression and of danger in anxiety, and the recognition of characteristic cognitive distortions, as outlined in Chapter 1. These additional levels of analysis allow the counsellor not only to be able to recognise negative automatic thoughts themselves but also to begin to help the client recognise them and their themes and distortions, thereby starting to open out a way to change some of the negative thoughts. Another crucial concept is that of the domain of the thoughts, highlighted by both Beck and Ellis: the three sets of cognitions involving views of the self, of others and the world. Beck presents a slight variation on this in his concept of the cognitive triad in depression. The role of self-concept and its crucial effect on psychological health, disturbance and change has been noted in many theories of therapy such as those of Rogers and Winnicott. Self-concept may well be one of the crucial 'common factors' which tend to even out the effectiveness of different therapies (Raimy, 1975). The counsellor will therefore become very aware of negative thinking in relation to self-concept and will have some tools to work on that with the client.

In working with negative automatic thoughts in an eclectic way, it is important not to be over-simplistic about the meaning of the client's thoughts. An important aspect of how clients refer to their psychological processes is that it seems to be a natural human tendency to use short-hand language to describe our psychological functioning, especially when we are emotionally aroused. For example, we might say, 'Everyone at work criticises me all the time, they make me feel worthless.' In fact, the experience we are actually trying to convey may actually be more like, 'At work, there are twenty people, two of them are critical of me. It's only two, but they are significant players. One is continuously critical and the other only sometimes. The others are okay . . . but then they don't defend me . . . although some of them are quite sympathetic afterwards. Sometimes the criticisms just bounce off me but sometimes, like today, it really upsets me and I end up feeling down, angry and frustrated.' We can look back now and see that the former version is an exaggerated short-hand form.

We need these forms because it would take forever to explain anything if we strove too hard for accuracy and we also need people listening to understand the full impact of our upsetting experience.

Both Ellis (1962) and Beck (1976) have referred to these two streams of thinking which seem to run alongside each other – in Ellis' parlance, 'the sane sentence and the insane sentence', and, in Beck's, 'parallel trains of thought'. Tapping into these internal dialogues is the first stage of developing cognitively oriented work. If, however, the counsellor does not appreciate that there are *two* trains of thought, he is likely to get into some very unsubtle and disputatious lines of 'persuasion' with the client – thus fulfilling the stereotype of the bad (that is, dogmatically didactic) cognitive therapist.

At the level of using cognitive methods in an eclectic way, interventions may be carried out on an occasional basis as a response to particular passages in the client's narrative. There is, as yet, no attempt to pull these sequences into an overall structural intervention or case conceptualisation. Such a conceptualisation would be the hallmark of a more concerted attempt to apply the whole model of cognitive counselling and it is to this that we now turn.

Level Two – Use of the Cognitive Model as the Main Approach

For counsellors who decide to take up the cognitive model in a major way, often one of its main positive points to the trainee is that it can give a feeling of expertise in recognising a specific issue for which one has a tried and tested intervention – 'If you've ever wondered what can I do with this client next, then cognitive counselling could be the one for you', as one of our students recently put it. This puts the model in stark contrast to others – particularly the 'growth'-oriented therapies such as person-centred and Gestalt therapy, and therapies focused on longer-term personality change, such as psychodynamic psychotherapy. We are not arguing that cognitive counselling is best confined to arenas like the NHS but that its emphasis within independent practice would probably be geared towards working in more specific contexts than growth work (John Jones, personal communication, 1996).

In order to begin to operate the full model in practice, one would need to practise using the structure laid out in the earlier chapters of this book. One really should learn the model inside out before experimentally changing it. Such adherence to structure is sometimes difficult for experienced counsellors and those brought up in less structured traditions. One should also begin by learning to use standard cognitive therapy before beginning to attempt schema-focused cognitive therapy. In some ways schema-focused cognitive therapy is more 'sexy' than the standard version. The emphasis on early experience and the therapeutic alliance in schema-focused work may make it seem more profound. The reason why it is important to master the standard model first is that it is the more parsimonious version – it is specifically short term. If we were to go 'schema-hunting' with all our clients then we may eventually be drawn into a much less effective and parsimonious way of working. Indeed, Beck (1994) observed that analysis of some session records show that more experienced therapists may do less effective cognitive therapy than do the less experienced: process analysis of sessions seemed to suggest that the more experienced therapists appeared to give themselves more licence to wander from the formal structure of the therapy.

Counsellors may well seek to combine cognitive ways of working with other ways of working before they have specialist training in cognitive therapy. At the pre-specialist training stage, combinations would be in the more eclectic mode: that is, they would not be guided by any over-arching theoretical integration or by any case conceptualisation. At the post-specialist stage, combinations would be made in a more explicitly theoretical integrative way (Norcross and Arkowitz, 1992), guided by a clear model of case conceptualisation.

Level Three – Using Structured Cognitive Interventions Eclectically and Integratively with Other Approaches

Beck has consistently argued that cognitive therapy is not a technique-driven approach. Many techniques, including those of diverse therapies can be used legitimately within cognitive therapy, provided that they are congruent with a genuinely cognitive case conceptualisation. He further argues that because the change generated by all therapies is essentially cognitive, cognitive therapy could prove to be *the* integrative therapy. In a recent publication (Beck, 1996), he even expresses the hope that cognitive therapy will melt away as a separate therapy as many of its methods will come to be regarded as standard for psycho-therapy.

The subject of integration is a potentially huge one and, for the purpose of this book, we wish to make a limited foray into this area by looking at two strongly developing directions in cognitive therapy. The first is the use of experientially oriented techniques, predominantly from the humanistic therapies, alongside cognitive work. The second is the renaissance of interest in the therapeutic alliance, a concept which owes so much to the psychodynamic therapies.

EXPERIENTIAL INFLUENCES   We have already referred to the real-isation that there was a gap in the way that the earlier models of cognitive therapy dealt with emotion. It has now become absolutely clear that cognitive therapy can only have a very limited effect if it does not tap into key emotional experiences. The search is therefore now on to incorporate experiential techniques into cognitive therapy, in particular the notion of staying with emotion and the use of imagery.

In Rogerian therapy, there has always been a recognition of the need to stay with and respect emotional experience. To some extent, this was acknowledged in the initial formulations of cognitive therapy, mainly in order to foster emotional change or symptom relief. One surprising gap in Beck's work has been the lack of emphasis on grieving processes. This is especially so as the theme of loss is so clearly identified in the cognitive therapy of depression yet merits no reference in the index of the landmark 1979 book on the subject (Beck et al., 1979). The impression is heightened by Beck's session on the well-known 'Richard' video tape, where Richard briefly mentions that his grandmother is dying. Admittedly, Richard himself does not think that it has a significant link to his current depression and yet many counsellors watching that moment consider that it might have been useful to stay with it just a little longer. More reflective work on grief might be a useful way to find what may be learned and added into cognitive therapy. Stirling Moorey (1996) shows that cognitive therapy can be used to support clients struggling with adjustment reactions to adverse life circumstances, such as grief reactions. Where adjustment of objectively negative circumstances is aimed for, the focus of cognitive therapy may well need to be more on facilitating emotional processing than on challenging negative thinking.

In addition to the concern in cognitive therapy to find new ways of advancing the emotional immediacy of our work, there is also a new interest in working with imagery, already referred to in Chapter 6. David Edwards (1989, 1990) has been exploring the use of Gestalt concepts and methods in this respect. Having obtained an image from the client, the therapist aims to reach the meanings which might be represented in the image. From a cognitive perspective, this offers the possibility that imagery work could be implemented along the same therapeutic track as the more usual verbal, cognitive interventions. Edwards notes the similarities between imagery work in cognitive therapy and Gestalt, illustrating his work with examples from Perls. The Gestaltist would help the client to understand that many features of the dream or image are projections of the client's own experiences and would typically ask the client to be that projection. As is often the case when comparing the cognitive approach with others, we are comparing an appreciation of a mental representation of a psychological feature in cognitive work with the acting out or experiencing of that feature in the other approach. The Gestalt approach in this instance would be more likely to promote emotional engagement with the client, whereas the cognitive approach might be more likely to promote a 'decentring' or 'distancing' (Safran and Segal, 1990) from the emotionally dysfunctional structure. One can imagine that there could be instances in which either of these therapeutic approaches would be more likely to be change-promoting for particular clients or even for the same client at different points in the process. Finally, some kind of combination of the approaches might prove helpful to some clients.

THE THERAPEUTIC ALLIANCE, TRANSFERENCE AND COUNTERTRANS-FERENCE   As cognitive therapy has developed and advanced, the therapeutic alliance has moved centre stage. It is in this area that the integration of cognitive therapy and other therapeutic disciplines becomes prominent. One example is in the way in which cognitive therapy is beginning to recognise and use the concepts of transference and countertransference, as discussed in Chapters 3 and 7.

The ideas of 'transference' and 'countertransference' were for so long such a taboo in cognitive-behavioural work that one still detects a sense of unease when cognitive therapists admit that it has crept back into their vocabulary. In their review of the interpersonal process and therapeutic relationship in cognitive therapy, Safran and Segal (1990) draw heavily on both the experiential therapies and the more recent versions of psychodynamic therapy. They base their analysis on the idea that clients exercise a characteristic 'interpersonal pull' in their relationships outside therapy. They will also bring this tendency to exercise pull into the therapeutic relationship. A frequently encountered example is when a client seeks continual reassurance from people around him and, perhaps, especially from the therapist. A counsellor working with a client who seeks frequent reassurance will often find herself looking at how the client seeks reassurance in his relationships. A cognitive counsellor may well wish to help the client review evidence on the health of such relationships. Bearing in mind that the client is likely to have developed skills in drawing out reluctant reassurance, any counsellor is likely to be drawn into responding to the client's requests for reassurance. However, the cognitive counsellor will be particularly 'hooked' by doing this. The first clue is often in the counsellor's countertransference to the client – most probably in the form of irritation. Recognising this countertransference is the first step in 'unhooking' oneself from this interpersonal trap. Once this is done, often with the help of supervision, the counsellor can then proceed to think how the unhooking can be used to best therapeutic advantage: for example, how would the client respond to 'here and now' immediacy such as a sharing of one's irritation delivered in a non-retaliatory way? Often the case conceptualisation is a good guideline to puzzling out the way forward (Persons, 1989). Any significant cognitions about critical others or avoidance of confrontations would need to be taken into account in the planning, timing and delivery of such an intervention.

It is interesting that so far there has been rather more interest in countertransference in cognitive therapy than in transference – of which, Beck et al. (1979) merely note that it should be dealt with as is any other negative automatic thought. The reasons for this underdeveloped interest in transference as compared to countertransference are likely to lie in the fact that cognitive therapy has always tried to take clients' perceptions seriously and respectfully. There may be fears that this respect might be undermined by attributing unconscious motives more explanatory power than the client's own conscious motives. Also cognitive therapists have been more likely to own their own less-than-perfect fallibility with clients in recent years and indeed have found their own tools for client analysis very useful in working on their own 'negative stuff' about therapy and clients. Such 'negative stuff' would include classic mustabatory NATs like, 'I must be able to help all my clients', and 'This client should show more thanks for my sincere efforts to help him'. Persons (1989) devotes a whole chapter to cognitive therapy for the cognitive therapist, including a telling list of therapist negative thoughts and their antidotes.

At present, such integration is a very young endeavour. Counsellors who have already undergone a substantial training in one of the cognitive therapies and have embedded this training into their practice can begin to think how they can undertake such integration themselves. Two main ways seem to arise in our own practice at this time. Firstly, some kind of gap in one's work with a particular client may become evident in supervision. For example, when working with clients who have great difficulty gaining access to truly visceral emotions, such access can be greatly facilitated by the use of techniques from Gestalt therapy. One client, Maggie, seemed to be paralysed by early memories of abusive parenting. Gaining access to visceral early memories via imagery and a modified version of the 'empty chair' technique allowed her to begin rapid processing of those memories. Secondly, one may identify, in supervision or otherwise, a persistent block about a particular client or group of clients within oneself. For example one client, Jim, reacted badly to any mention of goals and limits in therapy. Supervision helped me (FW) to see that, not only did he have a sensitivity to any prospect of ending counselling because to him it signalled a rejection, but that I was also reacting to a barely conscious fear of my own that I did not have the time and energy to help him.

Such integration is likely to be best fostered by collaborative work with colleagues with training in other disciplines. I (FW) have been lucky enough to have sustained contact, through supervision and other channels, with fellow therapists with training in both Gestalt (including the late and sorely missed John Jones) and psychodynamic therapy. Such arrangements require a committed effort to respect and learn from other disciplines. Mutual co-operation may have the additional benefit of fostering greater unity and integrity in the professions of counselling and psychotherapy in the potentially testing years as we go into the next millennium.

Conclusion

At whatever level the counsellor decides to try cognitive counselling, it is important that she is supported by good-quality supervision and training (Padesky, 1996). There are now a number of
training courses in cognitive therapy and cognitively-based counselling. The British Association of Behavioural and Cognitive
Psychotherapy (BABCP) is a good source of information on
courses, training events and sources of supervision. To some
extent, when contemplating taking on a model of therapy, the
counsellor has to decide if she wants to 'join the club' in terms of
training, conferences and supervision. We would like to end our
guide to cognitive counselling by suggesting that, if you do decide
to join the cognitive family, you are likely to find yourself welcomed to a group of people who are developing fast and are not
so serious that they can't be persuaded to mix some fun in with
the serious pursuit of therapy.

References

Abend, S.M., Border, M.S. and Willick, M.S. (1983) *Borderline Patients: Psychoanalytic Perspectives*. New York: International Universities Press.

Ainsworth, M.D.S. (1982) Attachment: Retrospect and prospect. In C.M. Parkes and J. Stevenson-Hinde (eds), *The Place of Attachment in Human Behaviour*. New York: Basic Books.

Alarcón, R.D. and Foulks, E.F. (1995) Personality disorders and culture: Contemporary clinical views. *Cultural Diversity and Mental Health*, 1 (1): 3–17.

American Psychiatric Association (1994) *Quick Reference to the Diagnostic Criteria from DSM-IV*. Washington, DC: American Psychiatric Association.

Bartlett, F.C. (1932) *Remembering*. New York: Columbia University Press.

Beck, A.T. (1964) Thinking and Depression: II: Theory and Practice. *Archives of General Psychiatry* 10: 561–71.

Beck, A.T. (1967) *Depression: Clinical, Experimental and Theoretical Aspects*. New York: Harper and Row.

Beck, A.T. (1970a) The role of fantasies in psychotherapy and psychopathology. *Journal of Nervous and Mental Disease*, 150: 3–17.

Beck, A.T. (1970b) Cognitive Therapy: Nature of Relation to Behavior Therapy. *Bahaviour and Therapy*, 1: 184–200.

Beck, A.T. (1976) *Cognitive Therapy and the Emotional Disorders*. New York: International Universities Press.

Beck, A.T. (1983) *Cognitive therapy of depression*: New perspectives. In P.J. Clayton and J.E. Barrett (eds), *Treatment of Depression: Old Controversies and New Approaches*. New York: Raven Press. pp. 265–84.

Beck, A.T. (1987) Cognitive models of depression. *Journal of Cognitive Psychotherapy: An International Quarterly*. 1 (1): 5–37.

Beck, A.T. (1988) *Love is Never Enough*. New York: Harper and Row.

Beck, A.T. (1991) Cognitive therapy as the integrative therapy. *Journal of Psychotherapy Integration*, 1: 191–8.

Beck, A.T. (1994) Address to the Oxford Branch of the British Association for Behavioural and Cognitive Psychotherapy, Warneford Hospital, Oxford.

Beck, A.T. (1996) Beyond belief: A theory of modes, personality and psychopathology. In P.M. Salkovskis (ed.), *Frontiers of Cognitive Therapy*. New York: Guilford Press. pp. 1–25.

Beck, A.T. and Steer, R.A. (1987) *Manual for the Revised Beck Depression Inventory*. San Antonio, TX: Psychological Corporation.

Beck, A.T. and Young, J.E. (1985) Depression. In D.H. Barlow (ed.), *Clinical Handbook of Psychological Disorders*. New York: Guilford Press. pp. 206–44.

Beck, A.T., Weissman, A., Lester, D. and Trexler, L. (1974a) The measurement of pessimism: The hopelessness scale. *Journal of Consulting and Clinical Psychology*, 42 (16): 861–5.

Beck, A.T., Schuyler, D. and Herman, I. (1974b) Development of suicide intent scales. In A.T. Beck, H.C.P. Resnik and D.J. Lettieri (eds), *The Prediction of Suicide.* Bowie, MD: Charles Press. pp. 45–56

Beck, A.T., Rush, A.J., Shaw, B.F. and Emery, G. (1979) *Cognitive Therapy of Depression.* New York: Guilford Press.

Beck, A.T., Emery, G. and Greenberg, R.L. (1985) *Anxiety Disorders and Phobias: A Cognitive Perspective.* New York: Basic Books.

Beck, A.T., Freeman, A. and Associates (1990) *Cognitive Therapy of Personality Disorders.* New York: Guilford Press.

Beck, A.T., Wright, F.D., Newman, C.F. and Liese, B.S. (1993) *Cognitive Therapy of Substance Abuse.* New York: Guilford Press.

Beck, J. (1995) *Cognitive Therapy: Basics and Beyond.* New York: Guilford Press.

Blackburn, I.M. (1987) *Coping with Depression.* Edinburgh: Chambers.

Blackburn, I.M. and Davidson, K. (1995) *Cognitive Therapy for Depression and Anxiety.* 2nd edn. Oxford: Blackwell Scientific Publications.

Bowlby, J. (1969) *Attachment and Loss. Volume 1: Attachment.* London: Hogarth Press and the Institute of Psychoanalysis.

Bowlby, J. (1973) *Attachment and Loss. Volume 2, Separation, Anxiety, and Anger.* New York: Basic Books.

Bowlby, J. (1980) *Attachment and Loss. Volume 3, Loss: Sadness and Depression.* London: Hogarth Press.

Bowlby, J. (1985) The role of childhood experience in cognitive disturbance. In M.J. Mahoney and A. Freeman (eds), *Cognition and Psychotherapy.* New York and London: Plenum. pp. 181–200.

Budman, S.H. and Gurman, A.S. (1988) *Theory and Practice of Brief Therapy.* London: Guilford Press.

Burns, D.D. (1980) *Feeling Good.* New York: New American Library.

Burns, D.D. (1989) *The Feeling Good Handbook.* New York: Plume.

Burns, D.D. and Nolen-Hoeksema, S. (1992) Therapeutic empathy and recovery from depression in cognitive behavioural therapy: A structural equation model. *Journal of Consulting and Clinical Psychology,* 60 (3): 441–9.

Butler, G. and Hope, T. (1996) *Manage your Mind.* Oxford: Oxford University Press.

Butler, G., Fennell, M., Robson, P. and Gelder, M. (1991) A comparison of behaviour therapy and cognitive therapy in the treatment of generalised anxiety disorder. *Journal of Consulting and Clinical Psychology,* 59: 167–75.

Carson, T.P. (1986) Assessment of depression. In A.R. Ciminero, K.S. Calhoun and H.E. Adams (eds), *Handbook of Behavioural Assessment.* 2nd edn. New York: John Wiley and Sons. pp. 404–45.

Casement, P. (1985) *On Learning from the Patient.* London: Tavistock.

Chambless, D.L., Caputo, G.C., Bright, P. and Gallagher, R. (1984) Assessment of fear of fear in agoraphobics: The Body Sensations Questionnaire and the Agoraphobic Cognitions Questionnaire. *Journal of Consulting and Clinical Psychology,* 52: 1090–7.

Clark, D.M. (1986) A cognitive approach to panic. *Behaviour Research and Therapy,* 24: 461–70.

Clark, D.M. (1989) Anxiety states: Panic and generalised anxiety. In K. Hawton, P.M. Salkovskis, J. Kirk and D.M. Clark (eds) *Cognitive Behaviour Therapy for Psychiatric Problems.* Oxford: Oxford University Press. pp. 52–96.

Clark, D.M. and Fairburn, C.G. (eds) (1996) *Science and Practice of Cognitive Behaviour Therapy.* Oxford: Oxford University Press.

Clark, D.M. and Wells, A. (1995) A cognitive model of social phobia. In R. Heimberg, D.A. Liebowitz, D.A. Hope and F.R. Schneier (eds), *Social Phobia: Diagnosis, Assessment and Treatment.* New York: Guilford Press. pp. 169–93.

Colarusso, C.A. and Nemiroff, R.A. (1981) *Adult Development.* New York: Plenum.

Coyne, J.L. and Gotlib, I. (1983) The role of cognitions in depression: A critical appraisal. *Psychological Bulletin,* 94: 472–505.

Day, R.W. and Sparacio, R.T (1989) Structuring the counselling process. In W. Dryden (ed.), *Key Issues for Counselling in Action.* London: Sage. pp. 16–25.

De Girolamo, G. and Reich, J.H. (1993) *Personality Disorders.* Geneva: World Health Organisation.

DeRubeis, R.J. and Feeley, M. (1990) Determinants of change in cognitive therapy for depression. *Cognitive Therapy and Research,* 14 (5): 469–82.

Dryden, W. (1982) *Social Problems: Treatment from a Rational-Emotive Perspective.* London: Institute for RET.

Dryden, W. (1984) *Individual Therapy in Britain.* Milton Keynes and Buckingham: Open University Press.

Dryden, W. (1987) *Counselling Individuals: The Rational-Emotive Approach.* London: Whurr.

Dryden, W. (1991) *A Dialogue with Albert Ellis: Against Dogmas.* Buckingham: Open University Press.

Dryden, W. (ed.) (1992) *Integrative and Eclectic Therapy: A Handbook.* Buckingham: Open University Press.

Dryden, W. and Feltham, C. (1992) *Brief Counselling.* Milton Keynes and Buckingham: Open University Press.

Dryden, W. and Feltham, C. (1994) *Developing the Practice of Counselling.* London: Sage.

Dryden, W. and Trower, P. (1988) *Developments in Cognitive Psychotherapy.* London: Sage.

Edwards, D.J.A. (1989) Cognitive restructuring through guided imagery: Lessons from Gestalt Therapy. In A. Freeman, K.M. Simon, L. Beutler and H. Arkowitz (eds), *Comprehensive Handbook of Cognitive Therapy.* New York: Plenum Press. pp. 283–97.

Edwards, D.J.A. (1990) Cognitive therapy and the restructuring of early memories through guided imagery. *Journal of Cognitive Psychotherapy: An International Quarterly,* 4 (1): 33–50.

Ellis, A. (1962) *Reason and Emotion in Psychotherapy.* Secaucus, NJ: Lyle Stuart.

Erikson, E.H. (1963) *Childhood and Society.* New York: W.W. Norton.

Evans, M.D., Hollon, S.D., DeRubeis, R.J., Piasecki, J.M., Grove, W.M., Garvey, M.J. and Tuason, V.B. (1992) Differential relapse rates following cognitive therapy and pharmacotherapy for depression. *Archives of General Psychiatry,* 49: 802–8.

Fairburn, C.G. and Cooper, P. (1989) Eating disorders. In K. Hawton, P.M. Salkovskis, J. Kirk and D.M. Clark (eds), *Cognitive Behaviour Therapy for Psychiatric Problems.* Oxford: Oxford University Press. pp. 277–314.

Fennell, M.J.V. (1989) Depression. In K. Hawton, P.M. Salkovskis, J. Kirk and D.M. Clark (eds), *Cognitive Behaviour Therapy for Psychiatric Problems.* Oxford: Oxford University Press. pp. 169–234.

Foa, E.B. and Kozak, M.J. (1986) Emotional processing of fear: Exposure to corrective information. *Psychological Bulletin*, 99: 20–35.

Fowler, D., Garety, P. and Kuipers, E. (1995) *Cognitive Behaviour Therapy for Psychosis*. Chichester: John Wiley and Sons.

Freeman, A. (1992) The development of treatment conceptualisations in cognitive therapy. In A. Freeman and F.M. Dattilio (eds), *Comprehensive Casebook of Cognitive Therapy*. New York: Plenum Press. pp. 13–23.

Freeman, A., Pretzer, J., Fleming, B. and Simon, K. (1990) *Clinical Applications of Cognitive Therapy*. New York: Plenum Press.

Gath, D. and Mynors-Wallis, L (1996) Problem solving treatment in primary care. In D.M. Clark and C.G. Fairburn (eds), *Science and Practice of Cognitive Behaviour Therapy*. Oxford: Oxford University Press. pp. 415–31.

Gilbert, P. (1984) *Depression: From Psychology to Brain State*. London: Lawrence Erlbaum Associates.

Gilbert, P. (1989) *Human Nature and Suffering*. London: Lawrence Erlbaum Associates.

Gilbert, P. (1992a) *Depression: The Evolution of Powerlessness*. London: Lawrence Erlbaum Associates.

Gilbert, P. (1992b) *Counselling for Depression*. London: Sage.

Greenberg, L.S. and Safran, J.D. (1984) Integrating affect and cognition: A perspective on the process of therapeutic changes. *Cognitive Therapy and Research*, 8: 559–78.

Greenberg, L.S. and Safran, J.D (1987) *Emotion in Psychotherapy. Affect, Cognition and the Process of Change*. New York: Guilford Press.

Greenberger, D. and Padesky, C. (1995) *Mind Over Mood*. New York: Guilford Press.

Guidano, V.F. (1991) *The Self in Process: A Developmental Approach to Psychotherapy and Therapy*. New York: Guilford Press.

Guidano, V.F. and Liotti, G. (1983) *Cognitive Processes and Emotional Disorders*. New York: Guilford Press.

Hamilton, M. (1960) A rating scale for depression. *Journal of Neurology, Neurosurgery and Psychiatry*, 12: 56–62.

Hawton, K., Salkovskis, P.M., Kirk, J. and Clark, D.M. (eds) (1989) *Cognitive Behaviour Therapy for Psychiatric Problems*. Oxford: Oxford University Press.

Hays, P.A. (1995) Multicultural applications of cognitive-behaviour therapy. *Professional Psychology: Research and Practice*, 26 (3): 309–15.

Hobson, R.F. (1985) *Forms of Feeling: The Heart of Psychotherapy*. London: Tavistock.

Holmes, J. (1993) *John Bowlby and Attachment Theory*. London: Routledge.

Horvath, A.O. (1995) The therapeutic relationship: From transference to alliance. *In Session: Psychotherapy in Practice*, 1 (1): 7–17.

Ivey, A E., Ivey, M.B. and Simek-Downing, L. (1987) *Counselling and Psychotherapy: Integrating Skills, Theory and Practice*. Englewood Cliffs, NJ: Prentice Hall International.

Jacobs, M. (1988) *Psychodynamic Counselling in Action*. London: Sage.

Jacobson, N.S. (1989) The therapist–client relationship in cognitive behaviour therapy: Implications for treating depression. *Journal of Cognitive Psychotherapy: An International Quarterly*, 3 (2): 85–96.

Kahn, M. (1991) *Between Therapist and Client: The New Relationship*. New York: W.H. Freeman and Co.

Kelly, G.A. (1955) *The Theory of Personal Constructs*. New York: W.W. Norton.

Kiesler, D.J. (1988) *Therapeutic Metacommunication: Therapist Impact Disclosure as Feedback in Psychotherapy*. Palo Alto, CA: Consulting Psychologists Press.

Kirk, J. (1989) Cognitive behavioural assessment. In K. Hawton, P.M. Salkovskis, J. Kirk and D.M. Clark (eds), *Cognitive Behaviour Therapy for Psychiatric Problems*. Oxford: Oxford University Press. pp. 13–51.

Kirschenbaum, H. and Henderson, V.L. (eds) (1990) *The Carl Rogers Reader*. London: Constable.

Layden, M.A., Newman, C.F., Freeman, A. and Morse, S.B. (1993) *Cognitive Therapy of Borderline Personality Disorder*. Boston: Allyn and Bacon.

Lazarus, R.S. (1980) Cognitive behaviour therapy as psychodynamics revisited. In M.J. Mahoney (ed.), *Psychotherapy Process: Current Issues and Future Directions*. New York: Plenum Press. pp. 121–6.

Ley, P. (1978) Memory for medical information. In M.M. Gruneberg, P.E. Morris and R.N. Sykes (eds), *Practical Aspects of Memory*. London: Academic Press. pp. 226–59.

Linehan, M.M. (1987) Dialectical behaviour therapy for borderline personality disorder: Theory and method. *Bulletin of the Menninger Clinic*, 51: 261–76.

Liotti, G. (1987) The resistance to change of cognitive structures: A counterproposal to psychoanalytic metapsychology. *Journal of Cognitive Psychotherapy*, 2: 87–104.

Liotti, G. (1991) Patterns of attachments and the assessment of interpersonal schemata: Understanding and changing difficult patient–therapist relationships in cognitive psychotherapy. *Journal of Cognitive Psychotherapy: An International Quarterly*, 5 (2): 105–14.

Mearns, D. and Dryden, W. (eds) (1990) *Experiences of Counselling in Action*. London: Sage.

Moore, T. (1992) *Care of the Soul: How to Add Depth and Meaning to Everyday Life*. London: Piatkus.

Moorey, S. (1996) When bad things happen to rational people: Cognitive therapy in adverse life circumstances. In P. Salkovskis (ed.), *Frontiers of Cognitive Therapy*. New York: Guilford Press. pp. 450–69.

Nesse, R.M. and Williams, G.C. (1995) *Evolution and Healing: The New Science of Darwinian Medicine*. London: Weidenfeld and Nicolson.

Newman, C.F. (1994) Understanding client resistance: Methods for enhancing motivation to change. *Cognitive and Behavioural Practice*, 1: 47–69.

Norcross, J.C. and Arkowitz, H. (1992) The evolution and current status of psychotherapy integration. In W. Dryden (ed.), *Integrative and Eclectic Therapy: A Handbook*. Buckingham: Open University Press. pp. 1–40.

Overholser, J.C. (1993a) Elements of the Socratic method: I. Systematic questioning. *Psychotherapy*, 30 (1): 67–74.

Overholser, J.C. (1993b) Elements of the Socratic method: II. Inductive reasoning. *Psychotherapy*, 30 (1): 75–85.

Padesky, C.A. (1993a) Socratic questioning: Changing minds or guiding discovery? Keynote address to European Congress of Behavioural and Cognitive Therapies, London.

Padesky, C.A. (1993b) Schema as self prejudice. *International Cognitive Therapy Newsletter*, 5/6: 16–17.

Padesky, C.A. (1994) Schema change processes in cognitive therapy. *Clinical Psychology and Psychotherapy*, 1 (5): 267–78.

Padesky, C.A. (1996) Developing cognitive therapist competency: Teaching and supervision models. In P. Salkovskis (ed.), *Frontiers of Cognitive Therapy*. New York: Guilford Press. pp. 266–92.

Padesky, C.A. and Greenberger, D. (1995) *A Clinician's Guide to Mind Over Mood*. New York: Guilford Press.

Padesky, C.A. and Mooney, K. (1990) Clinical tip: Presenting the cognitive model to clients. *International Cognitive Therapy Newsletter*, 6: 13–14.

Palmer, S. and Szymonska, K. (1995) An introduction to cognitive therapy and counselling. *Counselling*, November: 302–6. Rugby: BAC Publications.

Persons, J.B. (1989) *Cognitive Therapy in Practice: A Case Formulation Approach*. New York: W.W. Norton.

Persons, J.B. (1993) Case conceptualisation in cognitive behaviour therapy. In K.T. Kuehlwein and H. Rosen (eds), *Cognitive Therapies in Action: Evolving Innovative Practice*. San Francisco: Jossey-Bass. pp. 33–53.

Persons, J.B. and Burns, D.D. (1985) Mechanisms of action in cognitive therapy: The relative contributions of technical and interpersonal interventions. *Cognitive Therapy and Research*, 9: 539–57.

Persons, J.B., Burns, D.D. and Perloff, J.M. (1988) Predictors of dropout and outcome in cognitive therapy for depression in a private practice setting. *Cognitive Therapy and Research*, 12 (6): 557–75.

Piaget, J. (1952) *The Origins of Intelligence in Children*. New York: International Universities Press.

Power, M.J. (1991) Cognitive science and behavioural psychotherapy: Where behaviour was, there cognition shall be? *Behavioural Psychotherapy*, 19: 20–41.

Prochaska, J.O. and DiClemente, C.C. (1984) *The Transtheoretical Approach*. Homewood, IL: Dow Jones-Irwin.

Raimy, V. (1975) *Misunderstandings of the Self*. San Francisco: Jossey-Bass.

Raue, P.J. and Goldfried, M.R. (1994) The therapeutic alliance in cognitive behaviour therapy. In A.O. Horvath and L.S. Greenberg (eds), *The Working Alliance*. New York: John Wiley and Sons. pp. 131–52.

Rogers, C.R. (1957) The necessary and sufficient conditions of therapeutic personality change. *Journal of Consulting and Clinical Psychology*, 21: 95–103.

Ryle, A. (1990) *Cognitive-Analytic Therapy: Active Participation in Change: A New Integration in Brief Psychotherapy*. Chichester and New York: John Wiley and Sons.

Safran, J.D. (1990) Towards a refinement of cognitive therapy in the light of interpersonal theory. Parts 1 and 2. *Clinical Psychology Review*, 10: 87–121.

Safran, J.D. and Greenberg, L.S. (1988) Feeling, thinking and acting: A cognitive framework for psychotherapy integration. *Journal of Cognitive Psychotherapy: An International Quarterly*, 5 (13): 109–31.

Safran, J.D. and Segal Z.V. (1990) *Interpersonal Processes in Cognitive Therapy*. New York: Basic Books.

Safran, J.D., Segal Z.V., Vallis, T.M., Shaw, B.F. and Samstag, L.W. (1993) Assessing patient suitability for short-term cognitive therapy with an interpersonal focus. *Cognitive Therapy and Research*, 17 (1): 23–38.

Salkovskis, P. (1985) Obsessional-compulsive problems: A cognitive behavioural analysis. *Behaviour Research and Therapy*, 25: 571–83.

Salkovskis, P.M. (1989) Somatic problems. In K. Hawton, P.M. Salkovskis, J. Kirk and D.M. Clark (eds), *Cognitive Behaviour Therapy for Psychiatric Problems*. Oxford: Oxford University Press. pp. 235–76.

Salkovskis, P.M. (1991) The importance of behaviour in the maintenance of panic and anxiety: A cognitive account. *Behavioural Psychotherapy*, 19: 6–19.

Salkovskis, P.M. (1996) Avoidance behaviour is motivated by threat beliefs: A possible resolution of the cognition–behaviour debate. In P.M. Salkovskis (ed.), *Trends in Cognitive and Behavioural Therapies*. New York: John Wiley and Sons. pp. 25–41.

Salkovskis, P. and Bass, C. (1996) Hypochondriasis. In D.M. Clark and C.G. Fairburn (eds), *Science and Practice of Cognitive Behaviour Therapy*. Oxford: Oxford University Press. pp. 313–39.

Salkovskis, P.M. and Kirk, J. (1989) Obsessive-compulsive disorder. In K. Hawton, P.M. Salkovskis, J. Kirk and D.M. Clark (eds), *Cognitive-Behaviour Therapy for Psychiatric Problems: A Practical Approach*. Oxford: Oxford University Press. pp. 129–68.

Salkovskis, P., Richards, H.C. and Forrester, E. (1995) The relationship between obsessional problems and intrusive thoughts. *Behavioural and Cognitive Psychotherapy*, 23 (3): 281–99.

Salkovskis, P.M., Clark, D.M. and Gelder, M.G. (1996) Cognition–behaviour links in the persistence of panic. *Behaviour Research and Therapy*, 34: 453–8.

Sanders, D. (1996) *Counselling for Psychosomatic Problems*. London: Sage.

Scott, J. (1992) Chronic depression: Can cognitive therapy succeed when other treatments fail? *Behavioural Psychotherapy*, 20: 63–72.

Scott, M.J. and Stradling, S.G. (1990) Group cognitive therapy for depression produces clinically significant reliable change in community-based settings. *Behavioural Psychotherapy*, 18: 1–19.

Scott, M.J. and Stradling, S.G. (1992) *Counselling for Post-Traumatic Stress Disorder*. London: Sage.

Scott, M.J., Stradling, S.G. and Dryden, W. (1995) *Developing Cognitive Behavioural Counselling*. London: Sage.

Shea, M.T., Elkin, I., Imber, S T., Sotsky, S.M., Watkins, J.T., Collins, J.F., Pilonis, P.A., Beckham, E., Glass, D.R., Dolan, R.T. and Parloff, M.B. (1992) Course of depressive symptoms over follow up: Findings from the National Institute of Mental Health treatment of depression collaborative research program. *Archives of General Psychiatry*, 49: 782–7.

Sroufe, L.A. (1979) Socioemotional development. In J.D. Osofsky (ed.), *Handbook of Infant Development*. New York: John Wiley and Sons.

Stern, D.N. (1985) *The Interpersonal World of the Infant*. New York: Basic Books.

Stevens, A. and Price, J. (1996) *Evolutionary Psychiatry: A New Beginning*. London: Routledge.

Strupp, H.H. and Binder, J.L. (1984) *Psychotherapy in a New Key*. New York: W.W. Norton.

Sullivan, H.S. (1953) *The Interpersonal Theory of Psychiatry*. New York: W.W. Norton.

Surawy, C., Hackmann, A., Hawton, K. and Sharpe, M. (1995) Chronic fatigue syndrome: A cognitive approach. *Behaviour Research and Therapy*, 33 (5): 535–44.

Taylor, S.E. (1983) Adjustment to threatening events: A theory of cognitive adaptation. *American Psychologist*, 38 (11): 1161–73.

Teasdale, J. (1996) The relationship between cognition and emotion: The mind-in-place mood disorders. In D.M. Clark and C.G. Fairburn (eds), *Science and Practice of Cogntive Behaviour Therapy*. Oxford: Oxford University Press. pp. 67–93.

Turkat, I.D. and Carlson, C.R. (1984) Data-based versus symptomatic formulation of treatment: The case of a dependent personality. *Journal of Behaviour Therapy and Experimental Psychiatry*, 15: 153–60.

Turkat, I.D. and Maisto, S.A. (1985) Personality disorders: Application of the experimental method to the formulation and modification of personality disorders. In D.H. Barlow (ed.), *Clinical Handbook of Psychological Disorders*. New York: Guilford Press. pp. 502–70.

Van Nelzen, C.J.M. and Emmelkamp, P.M.G. (1996) The assessment of personality disorders: Implications for cognitive and behaviour therapy. *Behaviour Research and Therapy*, 34 (8): 655–68.

Ward, D.E. (1989) Termination of individual counselling: Concepts and strategies. In W. Dryden (ed.), *Key Issues for Counselling in Action*. London: Sage. pp. 97–110.

Weishaar, M.E. (1993) *Aaron. T. Beck*. London: Sage.

Weishaar, M.E. and Beck, A.T. (1992) Clinical and cognitive predictors of suicide. In R.W. Maris, A.L. Berman, J.T. Mattsberger and R.I. Yufit (eds), *Assessment and Prediction of Suicide*. New York: Guilford Press. pp. 467–83.

Wells, A. (1994) Attention and the control of worry. In G.C.L. Davey and F. Tallis (eds), *Worry: Perspective on Theory, Assessment and Treatment*. Chichester: John Wiley and Sons.

Wells, A. (1995) Meta-cognition and worry in generalised anxiety disorder. *Behavioural and Cognitive Psychotherapy*, 23 (3): 301–20.

Wells, A. (1996) *Cognitive Therapy of Anxiety Disorders: A Practical Guide*. Chichester: John Wiley and Sons.

Wells, A. and Butler, G. (1996) Generalised anxiety disorder. In D.M. Clark and C.G. Fairburn (eds), *Science and Practice of Cognitive Behaviour Therapy*. Oxford: Oxford University Press. pp. 155–78.

Wells, A. and Hackmann, A. (1993) Imagery and core beliefs in health anxiety: Content and origins. *Behavioural and Cognitive Psychotherapy*, 21(3): 265–74.

Wells, A. and Matthews, G. (1994) *Attention and Emotion: A Clinical Perspective*. Hove: Lawrence Erlbaum Associates.

Westbrook, D. (1993) Cutting waiting lists by cutting treatment: Outcome and pitfalls. Paper presented at European Congress of Behavioural and Cognitive Therapies, London.

Wills, F.R. (in press) Cognitive counselling: A down to earth and accessible therapy. In C. Sills (ed.), *Contracts in Counselling*. London: Sage.

Winnicott, D.W. (1965) *Maturational Processes and the Facilitating Environment*. London: Hogarth Press.

World Health Organisation (1993) *The ICD-10 Classification of Mental and Behavioural Disorders*. Geneva: World Health Organisation.

Wright, J.H. and Davis, D. (1994) The therapeutic relationship in cognitive behavioural therapy: Patient perceptions and therapist responses. *Cognitive and Behavioural Practice*, 1: 25–45.

Wright, J.H., Thase, M., Beck, A.T., and Ludgate, J.W. (eds) (1993) *Cognitive Therapy with Inpatients: Developing a Cognitive Milieu*. New York: Guilford Press.

Yalom, I.D. (1975) *The Theory and Practice of Group Psychotherapy*. 2nd edn. New York: Basic Books.

Young, J.E. (1994) *Cognitive Therapy for Personality Disorders: A Schema-Focused Approach*. 2nd edn. Sarasota, FL: Personal Resource Exchange.

Young, J.E. and Beck, A.T. (1980) *Cognitive Therapy Rating Scale Manual.* Philadelphia: Center for Cognitive Therapy, University of Pennsylvania.

Young, J.E. and Klosco, J.S. (1993) *Reinventing Your Life.* London: Penguin.

Zettle, R.D., Haflich, J.L. and Reynolds, R.A. (1992) Responsivity to cognitive therapy as a function of treatment format and client personality dimensions. *Journal of Clinical Psychology,* 48: 787–97.

Index